PRECEDENTS OF PLEADINGS

First Cumulative Supplement to the Fifteenth Edition

VOLUMES 1 AND 2

AUSTRALIA
Law Book Co.
Sydney

CANADA AND USA
Carswell
Toronto

HONG KONG
Sweet & Maxwell Asia

NEW ZEALAND
Brookers
Wellington

SINGAPORE AND MALAYSIA
Sweet & Maxwell Asia
Singapore and Kuala Lumpur

BULLEN & LEAKE & JACOB'S
PRECEDENTS OF PLEADINGS

FIRST CUMULATIVE SUPPLEMENT TO THE FIFTEENTH EDITION

VOLUMES 1 AND 2
General Editors

LORD BRENNAN Q.C.
A Barrister of Matrix Chambers, Gray's Inn
Chairman of the Bar, 1999

WILLIAM BLAIR Q.C.
A Barrister of 3 Verulam Buildings
Gray's Inn

Advisory Editors

SIR BRIAN LANGSTAFF
A Judge of the High Court, Queen's Bench Division
Formerly a Barrister of Cloisters Chambers, Temple

THE HONOURABLE SIR ROBIN JACOB
Judge of the Chancery Division of the High Court
Consulting Editor to Kerly's Law of Trade Marks and Trade Names
Advisory Editor to Civil Procedure 2000

WITH
SPECIALIST CONTRIBUTORS

LONDON
SWEET & MAXWELL
2005

Published in 2005 by
Sweet & Maxwell Limited of
100 Avenue Road, London NW3 3PF
www.sweetandmaxwell.co.uk
Typeset by Sweet & Maxwell Limited
Printed and bound in Great Britain by Athenaeum Press, Gateshead, Tyne & Wear

No natural forests were destroyed to make this product;
only farmed timber was used and replanted

A CIP catalogue record for this book is available from the British Library

ISBN 0421–903902

All rights reserved. Crown Copyright material is reproduced with the permission of the Controller of HMSO and the Queen's Printer for Scotland.
No part of this publication may be reproduced or transmitted, in any form or by any means, or stored in any retrieval system of any nature without prior written permission, except for permitted fair dealing under the Copyright, Designs and Patents Act 1988, or in accordance with the terms of a licence issued by the Copyright Licensing Agency in respect of photocopying and/or reprographic reproduction. Application for permission for other use of copyright material including permission to reproduce extracts in in other published works shall be made to the publishers. Full acknowledgement of author, publisher and source must be given.

The commentary and precedents contained in this publication are not tailored to any particular factual situation. They may be used as a guide for the drafting of legal documents but not otherwise reproduced. The publishers and the author cannot accept any responsibility for loss occasioned to any person acting or refraining from action as a result of the material in this publication.

©
Sweet & Maxwell Limited
2005

SPECIALIST CONTRIBUTORS

ASSAULT, FALSE IMPRISONMENT & MALICIOUS PROSECUTION

PAUL SPENCER
a Barrister of Cloisters Chambers
Temple

AVIATION

AKHIL SHAH, M.A.
a Barrister of Fountain Court Chambers
Temple

Carriage by Air

PAUL SINCLAIR, LL.M. (HARV), M.A. (CANTAB)
a Barrister of Fountain Court Chambers
Temple

Aviation

BANKING & FINANCIAL SERVICES

RICHARD DE LACY Q.C. M.A. (CANTAB), F.C.I.ARB.
of the Middle Temple and a Barrister of 3 Stone Buildings
Lincoln's Inn

Equitable Remedies
Financial Services
Sale of Shares
Stock Exchange

CATHERINE GIBAUD, B.BUS.SC. (HONS) (ACTUARIAL SC.) DIP.LAW (CITY)
a Barrister of 3 Verulam Buildings
Gray's Inn

Guarantees
Mortgages and Charges
Undue Influence

JONATHAN MARK PHILLIPS, B.A. (CANTAB)
a Barrister of 3 Verulam Buildings
Gray's Inn

Bills of Exchange
Cheques
Promissory Notes

IAN WILSON, M.A. (CANTAB), LL.M. (CANTAB)
a Barrister of 3 Verulam Buildings
Gray's Inn

Bankers
Bills of Sale
Bonds
Money Lent

BUSINESS LAW

RICHARD MAWREY Q.C. M.A.
a Barrister of Henderson Chambers
Temple

ANDREW KINNIER, M.A. (CANTAB)
a Barrister of Henderson Chambers
Temple

Commission Agents
Credit, Finance and Leasing
Factoring
Lien and Set-Off
Sale of Goods
Title to Goods—Torts Against Goods
Surety

COMPUTERS & I.T.

CLIVE FREEDMAN, M.A., F.C.I.ARB., FBCS
a Barrister of 3 Verulam Buildings
Gray's Inn

DEFAMATION

ANDREW CALDECOTT Q.C. B.A. (OXON)
a Barrister of 1 Brick Court
Temple

Libel and Slander
Malicious Falsehood

JANE PHILLIPS, B.A. (OXON)
a Barrister of 1 Brick Court
Temple

Libel and Slander
Malicious Falsehood

EDUCATION

PHILIP ENGLEMAN
a Barrister of Cloisters Chambers
Temple

EMPLOYMENT

JENNIFER EADY, B.A. (OXON), DIP.LAW
a Barrister of Old Square Chambers
Gray's Inn

Industrial Action

PAUL MICHELL, M.A. (CANTAB)
a Barrister of Cloisters Chambers
Temple

Employment Tribunal
Proceedings in the High Court and County Court

KARON MONAGHAN
a Barrister of Matrix Chambers
Gray's Inn

Harassment
Discrimination in Employment

ANTONY WHITE Q.C.
a Barrister of Matrix Chambers
Gray's Inn

Trade Unions

ENTERTAINMENT LAW

RICHARD EDWARDS, M.A., M.PHIL. (CANTAB)
a Barrister of 3 Verulam Buildings
Gray's Inn

ANDREW SUTCLIFFE Q.C. M.A. (OXON)
a Barrister of 3 Verulam Buildings
Gray's Inn
A Recorder of the Crown Court

ENVIRONMENTAL CLAIMS

MAURICE SHERIDAN
a Barrister of Matrix Chambers
Gray's Inn

FRAUD

JULIET MAY, M.A. (OXON), M.PHIL. (LOND)
a Barrister of 3 Verulam Buildings
Gray's Inn

NATALIE BAYLIS, M.A. (EDIN)
a Barrister of 3 Verulam Buildings
Gray's Inn

LAURA JOHN, B.A. (OXON)
a Barrister of 3 Verulam Buildings
Gray's Inn

HUMAN RIGHTS & REFERENCES TO THE ECJ

ROBIN ALLEN Q.C.
a Barrister of Cloisters Chambers
Temple
Former Chairman of the Employment Law Bar Association
Representative of the Bar Council on the Human Rights Task Force

Human Rights
References to the European Court of Justice

IMMIGRATION & JUDICIAL REVIEW

SAM GRODZINSKI
a Barrister of Matrix Chambers

STEVEN KOVATS
a Barrister of 39 Essex Street

Immigration
Judicial Review

INSURANCE

CHRISTOPHER SYMONS Q.C.
a Barrister of 3 Verulam Buildings
Gray's Inn
Deputy High Court Judge and Recorder of the Crown Court

RORY PHILLIPS Q.C. M.A.
a Barrister of 3 Verulam Buildings
Gray's Inn

TOM WEITZMAN Q.C. B.A. (OXON)
a Barrister of 3 Verulam Buildings
Gray's Inn

ELIZABETH BIRCH, LL.B., F.C.I.ARB.
a Barrister of 3 Verulam Buildings
Gray's Inn

JONATHAN DAVIES-JONES, M.A. (CANTAB)
a Barrister of 3 Verulam Buildings
Gray's Inn

SOPHIE MALLINCKRODT, M.A. (CANTAB)
a Barrister of 3 Verulam Buildings
Gray's Inn

INTELLECTUAL PROPERTY

JAMES ABRAHAMS, B.A., B.C.L.
a Barrister of 8 New Square
Lincoln's Inn

JESSIE BOWHILL, LL.B.
a Barrister of 8 New Square
Lincoln's Inn

MARK CHACKSFIELD, M.A. (CANTAB)
a Barrister of 8 New Square
Lincoln's Inn

JAMES MELLOR, M.A.
a Barrister of 8 New Square
Lincoln's Inn

PERSONAL INJURY

CHARLES CORY-WRIGHT
a Barrister of 39 Essex Street

Product Liability

CASPAR GLYN
a Barrister of Cloisters Chambers
Temple

Personal Injury
Employment

ROBIN OPPENHEIM
a Barrister of Doughty Street Chambers

Multi-Party Actions

KRISTINA STERN, PH.D. (CANTAB), B.A., LL.B. (HONS) (MELB)
a Barrister of 39 Essex Street

Clinical Negligence

PROFESSIONAL NEGLIGENCE

BRIAN DOCTOR Q.C., B.C.L., B.A., LL.B.
a Barrister of Fountain Court Chambers
Temple

PATRICK GOODALL, LL.B., B.C.L.
a Barrister of Fountain Court Chambers
Temple

GILLIAN KEENE, M.A. (OXON)
a Barrister of Farrar's Building
Temple

PATRICIA ROBERTSON, B.A. (OXON)
a Barrister of Fountain Court Chambers
Temple

DAVID WAKSMAN Q.C. LL.B., B.C.L.
Recorder of the Crown and County Courts

PROPERTY

JOHN CHERRYMAN, Q.C.
a Barrister of Landmark Chambers

STEPHEN BICKFORD-SMITH
a Barrister of Landmark Chambers

Distress and Replevin

CAMILLA LAMONT
a Barrister of Landmark Chambers

Landlord & Tenant—third party rights and obligations

ALISON OAKES
a Barrister of Landmark Chambers

Co-ownership
Easements and Drainage
Landlord & Tenant—repairs and improvements
Rights of Common
Landlord & Tenant—covenants against assignment
Landlord & Tenant—flats
Landlord & Tenant—other covenants
Landlord & Tenant—possession proceedings
Landlord & Tenant—protection from eviction
Landlord & Tenant—rent and service charges
Restrictive Covenants
Mesne Profits and Use and Occupation
Construction and Rent Review
Business Tenancies

NICHOLAS TAGGART
a Barrister of Landmark Chambers

Adverse Possession
Sale of Land
Fences, Boundaries and Access

MYRIAM STACEY
a Barrister of Landmark Chambers

Mortgages

KATE OLLEY
a Barrister of Landmark Chambers

Trespass

RESTITUTION

MARCUS SMITH, B.C.L., M.A. (OXON)
*a Barrister of Fountain Court Chambers
Temple*

HENRY KING, M.A. (OXON), A.C.A.
*a Barrister of Fountain Court Chambers
Temple*

SPORTS LAW

JONATHAN BELLAMY, M.A. (OXON)
a Barrister of 39 Essex Street

Publisher's Note

This is the first supplement to the fifteenth edition of *Bullen & Leake & Jacob's Precedents of Pleadings*. It is up to date generally to May 31, 2005.

Within each Chapter, updating information is referenced to the relevant paragraph in the Main Volume. The instructions in italics explain how the added material relates to the Main Volume.

Table of Cases

A v Leeds Teaching Hospital NHS Trust, *sub nom.* AB v Leeds Teaching Hospital NHS Trust; Organ Retention Group Litigation, Re [2004] EWHC 644; [2005] 2 W.L.R. 358; [2004] 2 F.L.R. 365; [2004] 3 F.C.R. 324; [2005] Lloyd's Rep. Med. 1; (2004) 77 B.M.L.R. 145; [2004] Fam. Law 501; (2004) 101(16) L.S.G. 28; (2004) 154 N.L.J. 497; *The Times*, April 12, 2004 37–02

—— (A Child) v Ministry of Defence [2004] EWCA Civ 641; [2005] Q.B. 183; [2004] 3 W.L.R. 469; [2004] P.I.Q.R. P35; [2004] Lloyd's Rep. Med. 351; (2004) 101(22) L.S.G. 32; *The Times*, May 17, 2004; *Independent*, May 13, 2004, CA (Civ Div); affirming [2003] EWHC 849; [2003] P.I.Q.R. P33; [2003] Lloyd's Rep. Med. 339; (2003) 100(26) L.S.G. 39; *The Times*, May 16, 2003 .... 72–04.1

AB v British Coal Corp [2004] EWHC 1372 37–02

—— v Leeds Teaching Hospital NHS Trust; Organ Retention Group Litigation, Re. *See* A v Leeds Teaching Hospital NHS Trust

A Fulton Co Ltd v Totes Isotoner (UK) Ltd [2003] EWCA Civ 1514; [2004] R.P.C. 16; (2004) 27(2) I.P.D. 27010; (2003) 147 S.J.L.B. 1306; *The Times*, November 19, 2003, CA (Civ Div); affirming [2003] R.P.C. 27 67–03

ASLEF v Lee, unreported, Febuary 24, 2004, EAT 34–08

Abbey National Plc v Boscawen. *See* Boscawen v Bajwa

Abu-Qulbain v Secretary of State for the Home Department; Kashmiri v Secretary of State for the Home Department. *See* Huang v Secretary of State for the Home Department

Actionstrength Ltd (t/a Vital Resources) v International Glass Engineering IN.GL.EN SpA [2003] UKHL 17; [2003] 2 A.C. 541; [2003] 2 W.L.R. 1060; [2003] 2 All E.R. 615; [2003] 2 All E.R. (Comm) 331; [2003] 1 C.L.C. 1003; [2003] B.L.R. 207; 88 Con. L.R. 208; (2003) 153 N.L.J. 563; (2003) 147 S.J.L.B. 418; *The Times*, April 4, 2003, HL; affirming [2001] EWCA Civ 1477; [2002] 1 W.L.R. 566; [2002] 4 All E.R. 468; [2002] C.L.C. 153; [2002] B.L.R. 44; [2002] T.C.L.R. 10; *Independent*, December 3, 2001 11–05

Adidas-Salomon AG v Fitnessworld Trading Ltd (C408/01) [2004] Ch. 120; [2004] 2 W.L.R. 1095; [2004] 1 C.M.L.R. 14; [2004] C.E.C. 3; [2004] E.T.M.R. 10; [2004] F.S.R. 21; *The Times*, October 31, 2003 [2003] E.T.M.R. 91 .... 68–01.1

Al-Fayed v Commissioner of Police of the Metropolis [2004] EWCA Civ 1579; (2004) 148 S.J.L.B. 1405, CA (Civ Div); affirming [2002] EWHC 1734 2–03

Alabaster v Barclays Bank Plc (formerly Woolwich Plc). *See* Alabaster v Woolwich Plc

—— v Woolwich Plc, *sub nom.* Alabaster v Barclays Bank Plc (formerly Woolwich Plc) [2005] EWCA Civ 508, CA (Civ Div); reversing [2000] I.C.R. 1037; [2000] I.R.L.R. 754; *The Times*, April 19, 2000 .... 35–01.2

Alfred McAlpine Plc v BAI (Run-Off) Ltd [2000] 1 All E.R. (Comm) 545; [2000] 1 Lloyd's Rep. 437; [2000] C.L.C. 812; (2001) 3 T.C.L.R. 5; 69 Con. L.R. 87; [2000] Lloyd's Rep. I.R. 352, CA (Civ Div); affirming [1998] 2 Lloyd's Rep. 694; [1998] C.L.C. 1145; (1999) 1 T.C.L.R. 92; 66 Con. L.R. 57 58–10

Ansul BV v Ajax Brandbeveiliging BV (C40/01) [2005] Ch. 97; [2004] 3 W.L.R. 1048; [2003] E.C.R. I-2439; [2003] E.T.M.R. 85; [2003] R.P.C. 40 68–11

Arscott v Coal Authority [2004] EWCA Civ 892; [2005] Env L.R. 6; (2004) 148 S.J.L.B. 880; [2004] N.P.C. 114, CA (Civ Div); affirming [2003] EWHC 1690 38–02

Athletic Union of Constantinople (AEK) v National Basketball Association (Application to Strike Out), *sub nom.* National Basketball Association v Athletic Union of Constantinople (AEK) (Application to Strike Out); Athletic Union of Constantinople v National Basketball Association (No.2) [2002] EWCA Civ 830; [2002] 1 W.L.R. 2863; [2002] 3 All E.R. 897; [2002] 2 All E.R. (Comm) 385; (2002) 99(29) L.S.G. 33; (2002) 146 S.J.L.B. 153; *The Times*, June 13, 2002; *Independent*, June 13, 2002 99–04

TABLE OF CASES

Attorney General of Hong Kong v Reid [1994] 1 A.C. 324; [1993] 3 W.L.R. 1143; [1994] 1 All E.R. 1; (1993) 143 N.L.J. 1569; (1993) 137 S.J.L.B. 251; [1993] N.P.C. 144; *The Times*, November 12, 1993; *Independent*, November 24, 1993 52–04

Axa General Insurance Ltd v Gottlieb [2005] EWCA Civ 112; [2005] 1 All E.R. (Comm) 445; *The Times*, March 3, 2005 58–09

Bakewell Management Ltd v Brandwood, *sub nom.* Brandwood v Bakewell Management Ltd [2004] UKHL 14; [2004] 2 A.C. 519; [2004] 2 W.L.R. 955; [2004] 2 All E.R. 305; [2004] R.T.R. 26; [2005] 1 P. & C.R. 1; [2004] 2 E.G.L.R. 15; [2004] 20 E.G. 168; [2004] 15 E.G.C.S. 104; (2004) 101(18) L.S.G. 34; (2004) 154 N.L.J. 553; (2004) 148 S.J.L.B. 418; [2004] N.P.C. 53; [2004] 2 P. & C.R. DG6; *The Times*, April 2, 2004; *Independent*, April 6, 2004, HL; reversing [2003] EWCA Civ 23; [2003] 1 W.L.R. 1429; [2003] R.T.R. 30; [2003] 1 P. & C.R. 27; [2003] 1 E.G.L.R. 17; [2003] 09 E.G. 198; [2003] 6 E.G.C.S. 146; (2003) 100(11) L.S.G. 33; [2003] N.P.C. 12; [2003] 1 P. & C.R. DG22; *The Times*, February 5, 2003; *Independent*, February 7, 2003, CA (Civ Div); affirming [2002] EWHC 472; [2003] J.P.L. 75; [2002] 14 E.G.C.S. 124; (2002) 99(19) L.S.G. 30; (2002) 146 S.J.L.B. 102; *The Times*, April 19, 2002 83–03

Bank of India v Christopher Morris [2005] EWCA Civ 693; [2005] B.C.C. 739; *The Times*, July 19, 2005, CA (Civ Div) 49–07

Banks v Ablex Ltd [2005] EWCA Civ 173; (2005) 149 S.J.L.B. 269; *The Times*, March 21, 2005. . . . . 54–02.1—54–02.2

Barrett v Enfield LBC [2001] 2 A.C. 550; [1999] 3 W.L.R. 79; [1998] 1 W.L.R. 277; [1999] 3 All E.R. 193; [1999] 2 F.L.R. 426; [1999] 2 F.C.R. 434; (1999) 1 L.G.L.R. 829; [1999] B.L.G.R. 473; (1999) 11 Admin. L.R. 839; [1999] Ed. C.R. 833; (1999) 2 C.C.L. Rep. 203; [1999] P.I.Q.R. P272; (1999) 49 B.M.L.R. 1; [1999] Fam. Law 622; (1999) 96(28) L.S.G. 27; (1999) 143 S.J.L.B. 183; *The Times*, June 18, 1999 , HL; reversing [1998] Q.B. 367; [1997] 3 W.L.R. 628; [1997] 3 All E.R. 171; [1997] 2 F.L.R. 167; [1997] 3 F.C.R. 145; (1998) 10 Admin. L.R. 230; (1997) 37 B.M.L.R. 16; [1997] Fam. Law 534; *The Times*, April 22, 1997 . . . . 2–06B

Barros Mattos Junior v MacDaniels Ltd, *sub nom.* Mattos Junior v MacDaniels Ltd; Barros Mattos Junior v General Securities & Finance Co Ltd [2004] EWHC 1188; [2005] 1 W.L.R. 247; [2004] 3 All E.R. 299; [2004] 2 All E.R. (Comm) 501; [2004] 2 Lloyd's Rep. 475 98–08

Barton v County Natwest Ltd, *sub nom.* County Natwest Ltd v Barton [2002] 4 All E.R. 494 (Note); [1999] Lloyd's Rep. Bank. 408; [1999] E.G.C.S. 103; (1999) 96(33) L.S.G. 31; *The Times*, July 29, 1999 11–12

Bolam v Friern Hospital Management Committee [1957] 1 W.L.R. 582; [1957] 2 All E.R. 118; [1955-95] P.N.L.R. 7; 101 S.J. 357 . . . . 72–04.1

Bolitho (Deceased) v City and Hackney HA [1998] A.C. 232; [1997] 3 W.L.R. 1151; [1997] 4 All E.R. 771; [1998] P.I.Q.R. P10; [1998] Lloyd's Rep. Med. 26; (1998) 39 B.M.L.R. 1; [1998] P.N.L.R. 1; (1997) 94(47) L.S.G. 30; (1997) 141 S.J.L.B. 238; *The Times*, November 27, 1997, HL; affirming [1993] P.I.Q.R. P334; [1993] 4 Med. L.R. 381. . . . . 72–04.1, 72–06

Bolivinter Oil SA v Chase Manhattan Bank NA [1984] 1 W.L.R. 392; [1984] 1 Lloyd's Rep. 251; (1984) 128 S.J. 153 8–05

Bongrain SA's Trade Mark Application (No.2134604) [2004] EWCA Civ 1690; [2005] E.T.M.R. 47; [2005] R.P.C. 14, CA (Civ Div); affirming [2003] EWHC 531 . . 68–10

Bonnard v Perryman [1891] 2 Ch. 269; [1891–94] All E.R. Rep. 965 28–27

Boscawen v Bajwa, *sub nom.* Abbey National Plc v Boscawen [1996] 1 W.L.R. 328; [1995] 4 All E.R. 769; (1995) 70 P. & C.R. 391; (1995) 92(21) L.S.G. 37; (1995) 139 S.J.L.B. 111; *The Times*, April 25, 1995; *Independent*, May 23, 1995 53–07

Brandwood v Bakewell Management Ltd. *See* Bakewell Management Ltd v Brandwood

British Horseracing Board Ltd v William Hill Organisation Ltd (C203/02) [2005] 1 C.M.L.R. 15; [2005] C.E.C. 68; [2005] E.C.D.R. 1; [2005] R.P.C. 13 [2004] Info. T.L.R. 315 . . . . 66–21—66–22, 66–28

British Telecommunications Plc v Communication Workers Union [2003] EWHC 937; [2004] I.R.L.R. 58 . . . . 33–08, 33–10

Brooks v Commissioner of Police of the Metropolis [2005] UKHL 24; [2005] 1 W.L.R. 1495; [2005] 2 All E.R. 489; (2005) 155 N.L.J. 653; *The Times*, April 26, 2005, HL; reversing [2002] EWCA Civ 407; *Daily Telegraph*, April 11, 2002 . . . . . . 2–01, 2–06B

Table of Cases

C v Middlesborough BC [2004] EWCA Civ 1746; [2005] 1 F.C.R. 76, CA (Civ Div); affirming [2004] EWHC 1386 2–01
Campbell v MGN Ltd. *See* Campbell v Mirror Group Newspapers Ltd
—— v Mirror Group Newspapers Ltd, *sub nom.* Campbell v MGN Ltd [2004] UKHL 22; [2004] 2 A.C. 457; [2004] 2 W.L.R. 1232; [2004] 2 All E.R. 995; [2004] E.M.L.R. 15; [2004] H.R.L.R. 24; [2004] U.K.H.R.R. 648; 16 B.H.R.C. 500; (2004) 101(21) L.S.G. 36; (2004) 154 N.L.J. 733; (2004) 148 S.J.L.B. 572; *The Times*, May 7, 2004; *Independent*, May 11, 2004, HL; reversing [2002] EWCA Civ 1373; [2003] Q.B. 633; [2003] 2 W.L.R. 80; [2003] 1 All E.R. 224; [2003] E.M.L.R. 2; [2003] H.R.L.R. 2; (2002) 99(42) L.S.G. 38; (2002) 146 S.J.L.B. 234; *The Times*, October 16, 2002; *Independent*, October 18, 2002, CA (Civ Div); reversing [2002] EWHC 499; [2002] E.M.L.R. 30; [2002] H.R.L.R. 28; (2002) 99(19) L.S.G. 28; (2002) 146 S.J.L.B. 107; *The Times*, March 29, 2002; *Daily Telegraph*, April 11, 2002 .... 65–01—65–02, 65–08—65–09, 65–11
—— v United Kingdom; Hartley v United Kingdom. *See* Fox v United Kingdom (A/182)
Campbell-James v Guardian Media Group [2005] EWHC 893; [2005] E.M.L.R. 24, QBD 28–48
Carisbrooke Shipping CV5 v Bird Port Ltd [2005] EWHC 1974, QBD (Admlty) 27–11
Cenir v Entry Clearance Officer [2003] EWCA Civ 572 57–05
Chagos Islanders v Attorney General [2004] EWCA Civ 997; *The Times*, September 21, 2004, CA (Civ Div); affirming [2003] EWHC 2222; *The Times*, October 10, 2003 37–02
Charterhouse Clinical Research Unit Ltd v Richmond Pharmacology Ltd (Defamatory Meaning) [2003] EWHC 1099 .... 29–02A
Chester v Afshar [2004] UKHL 41; [2005] 1 A.C. 134; [2004] 3 W.L.R. 927; [2004] 4 All E.R. 587; (2005) 81 B.M.L.R. 1; [2005] P.N.L.R. 14; (2004) 101(43) L.S.G. 34; (2004) 154 N.L.J. 1589; (2004) 148 S.J.L.B. 1215; *The Times*, October 19, 2004, HL; affirming [2002] EWCA Civ 724; [2003] Q.B. 356; [2002] 3 W.L.R. 1195; [2002] 3 All E.R. 552; [2002] Lloyd's Rep. Med. 305; (2002) 67 B.M.L.R. 66; (2002) 99(29) L.S.G. 33; (2002) 146 S.J.L.B. 167; *The Times*, June 13, 2002; *Daily Telegraph*, June 13, 2002, CA (Civ Div); affirming 72–04.1, 75–04
CHINAWHITE Trade Mark; Harrison's Trade Mark Application. *See* Harrison v Teton Valley Trading Co Ltd
Collins Stewart Ltd v Financial Times Ltd (No.1) [2004] EWHC 2337; [2005] E.M.L.R. 5; (2004) 101(43) L.S.G. 33; *The Times*, October 26, 2004 28–26
—— v Financial Times Ltd (No.2) [2005] EWHC 262 28–24
Commerzbank AG v Jones; Commerzbank AG v Price-Jones; Price-Jones v Commerzbank AG. *See* Jones v Commerzbank AG
Compagnie Noga D'Importation et D'Exportation SA v Australia & New Zealand Banking Group Ltd [2005] EWHC 225 .... 53–07.1
Cooper v Pure Fishing (UK) Ltd (formerly Outdoor Technology Group (UK) Ltd) [2004] EWCA Civ 375; [2004] 2 Lloyd's Rep. 518; [2004] 2 C.L.C. 412; [2005] E.C.C. 6; [2004] Eu. L.R. 664 .... 20–01.2
County Natwest Ltd v Barton. *See* Barton v County Natwest Ltd
Coys of Kensington (Sales) Ltd v McDonald; McDonald v Coys of Kensington Holdings Ltd. *See* Cressman v Coys of Kensington (Sales) Ltd
Credit Agricole Indosuez v Muslim Commercial Bank Ltd [2000] 1 All E.R. (Comm) 172; [2000] 1 Lloyd's Rep. 275; [2000] Lloyd's Rep. Bank. 1; [2000] C.L.C. 437 5–05
Cressman v Coys of Kensington (Sales) Ltd, *sub nom.* Coys of Kensington (Sales) Ltd v McDonald; McDonald v Coys of Kensington Holdings Ltd [2004] EWCA Civ 47; [2004] 1 W.L.R. 2775; (2004) 101(10) L.S.G. 29; (2004) 148 S.J.L.B. 182; *The Times*, February 13, 2004 98–01
Criterion Properties Plc v Stratford UK Properties LLC [2004] UKHL 28; [2004] 1 W.L.R. 1846; [2004] B.C.C. 570; (2004) 101(26) L.S.G. 27; (2004) 148 S.J.L.B. 760; [2004] N.P.C. 96; *The Times*, June 25, 2004, HL; affirming [2002] EWCA Civ 1883; [2003] 1 W.L.R. 2108; [2003] B.C.C. 50; [2003] 2 B.C.L.C. 129, CA (Civ Div); reversing [2002] EWHC 496; [2002] 2 B.C.L.C. 151 .... 5–12.1

Table of Cases

Crown Dilmun v Sutton [2004] EWHC 52; [2004] 1 B.C.L.C. 468; [2004] W.T.L.R. 497; (2004) 101(7) L.S.G. 34; *The Times*, February 5, 2004 53–06

Cumming v Chief Constable of Northumbria [2003] EWCA Civ 1844; [2004] A.C.D. 42; (2004) 101(4) L.S.G. 31; *The Times*, January 2, 2004 2–03

Customs and Excise Commissioners v Barclays Bank Plc [2004] EWCA Civ 1555; [2005] 1 W.L.R. 2082; [2005] 3 All E.R. 852; [2005] 1 Lloyd's Rep. 165; (2004) 154 N.L.J. 1831; (2004) 148 S.J.L.B. 1402; [2004] N.P.C. 175; *Independent*, December 2, 2004, CA (Civ Div); reversing [2004] EWHC 122; [2004] 1 W.L.R. 2027; [2004] 2 All E.R. 789; [2004] 1 All E.R. (Comm) 960; [2004] 1 Lloyd's Rep. 572; [2004] 2 C.L.C. 1; (2004) 101(7) L.S.G. 35; (2004) 154 N.L.J. 224; *The Times*, February 11, 2004 .... 5–01, 75–02

—— v Total Network SL, unreported, LTL 14/1/2005 50–02

Czarnikow-Rionda Sugar Trading Inc v Standard Bank London Ltd [1999] 1 All E.R. (Comm) 890; [1999] 2 Lloyd's Rep. 187; [1999] Lloyd's Rep. Bank. 197; [1999] C.L.C. 1148; *Independent*, June 14, 1999 (C.S.) 8–05

Daniel v Drew *See* Drew v Daniel

Daraydan Holdings Ltd v Solland International Ltd [2004] EWHC 622; [2005] Ch. 119; [2004] 3 W.L.R. 1106; [2004] W.T.L.R. 815; [2004] N.P.C. 49 52–04

Deep Vein Thrombosis and Air Travel Group Litigation, Re [2003] EWCA Civ 1005; [2004] Q.B. 234; [2003] 3 W.L.R. 956; [2004] 1 All E.R. 445; [2004] 1 All E.R. (Comm) 459; [2004] 1 Lloyd's Rep. 316; [2003] 2 C.L.C. 884; [2003] P.I.Q.R. P35; (2004) 76 B.M.L.R. 38; (2003) 100(35) L.S.G. 34; (2003) 147 S.J.L.B. 869; *The Times*, July 14, 2003; *Independent*, July 8, 2003, CA (Civ Div); affirming [2002] EWHC 2825; [2003] 1 All E.R. 935; [2003] 1 All E.R. (Comm) 418; (2003) 71 B.M.L.R. 82; *The Times*, January 17, 2003 4–06

Dennis v Ministry of Defence [2003] EWHC 793; [2003] Env L.R. 34; [2003] E.H.L.R. 17; [2003] 2 E.G.L.R. 121; [2003] J.P.L. 1577; [2003] 19 E.G.C.S. 118; (2003) 153 N.L.J. 634; [2003] N.P.C. 55; *The Times*, May 6, 2003 3–02

Dextra Bank &Trust Co Ltd v Bank of Jamaica [2002] 1 All E.R. (Comm) 193 ...... 5–11.1

Dorset Co. Ltd v Home Office [1970] A.C. 104 .... 2–06B

Douglas v Hello! Ltd (No.6) [2005] EWCA Civ 595; [2005] 4 All E.R. 128; [2005] E.M.L.R. 28; [2005] 2 F.C.R. 487; [2005] H.R.L.R. 27; (2005) 28(8) I.P.D. 28057; (2005) 155 N.L.J. 828; *The Times*, May 24, 2005; *Independent*, May 26, 2005, CA (Civ Div); reversing in part [2003] EWHC 786; [2003] 3 All E.R. 996; [2003] E.M.L.R. 31; (2003) 153 N.L.J. 595; *Independent*, June 16, 2003 (C.S.), Ch D.. 50–03, 51–12, 65–02, 65–08—65–09, 65–11

Drake Insurance Plc v Provident Insurance Plc, *sub nom.* Drake Insurance Plc (In Provisional Liquidation) v Provident Insurance Plc [2003] EWCA Civ 1834; [2004] Q.B. 601; [2004] 2 W.L.R. 530; [2004] 2 All E.R. (Comm) 65; [2004] 1 Lloyd's Rep. 268; [2004] 1 C.L.C. 574; [2004] R.T.R. 19; [2004] Lloyd's Rep. I.R. 277, CA (Civ Div); reversing [2003] EWHC 109; [2003] 1 All E.R. (Comm) 759; [2004] R.T.R. 11; [2003] Lloyd's Rep. I.R. 781; *Independent*, March 31, 2003 (C.S.) 58–06, 58–06.2

Drake Insurance Plc (In Provisional Liquidation) v ——. *See* Drake Insurance Plc v Provident Insurance Plc

Drew v Daniel, *sub nom.* Daniel v Drew [2005] EWCA Civ 507; [2005] 2 F.C.R. 365; [2005] W.T.L.R. 807; *The Times*, May 18, 2005, CA (Civ Div) 17–03

Drury v Secretary of State for the Environment, Food and Rural Affairs, *sub nom.* Secretary of State for the Environment, Food and Rural Affairs v Drury [2004] EWCA Civ 200; [2004] 1 W.L.R. 1906; [2004] 2 All E.R. 1056; [2004] 3 E.G.L.R. 85; [2004] 37 E.G. 142; (2004) 101(12) L.S.G. 35; (2004) 148 S.J.L.B. 269; [2004] N.P.C. 32; *The Times*, March 15, 2004; *Independent*, March 3, 2004 37–04

TABLE OF CASES

Dunnachie v Kingston upon Hull City Council, *sub nom.* Williams v Southampton Institute; Dawson v Stonham Housing Association; Kingston Upon Hull City Council v Dunnachie (No.1) [2004] UKHL 36; [2005] 1 A.C. 226; [2004] 3 W.L.R. 310; [2004] 3 All E.R. 1011; [2004] I.C.R. 1052; [2004] I.R.L.R. 727; (2004) 101(33) L.S.G. 34; (2004) 154 N.L.J. 1156; (2004) 148 S.J.L.B. 909; *The Times*, July 16, 2004; *Independent*, July 21, 2004, HL; reversing [2004] EWCA Civ 84; [2004] 2 All E.R. 501; [2004] I.C.R. 481; [2004] I.R.L.R. 287; (2004) 101(10) L.S.G. 27; (2004) 154 N.L.J. 248; (2004) 148 S.J.L.B. 233; *The Times*, February 26, 2004; *Independent*, February 18, 2004, CA (Civ Div); reversing [2003] I.C.R. 1294; [2003] I.R.L.R. 384; *The Times*, June 9, 2003 . . . . 31–03.4

Elguzouli-Daf v Commissioner of Police of the Metropolis, *sub nom.* McBrearty v Ministry of Defence [1995] Q.B. 335; [1995] 2 W.L.R. 173; [1995] 1 All E.R. 833; (1995) 7 Admin. L.R. 421; (1995) 145 N.L.J. 151; *The Times*, November 23, 1994 . . . . 2–06B

Ellison v Ministry of Defence, 81 B.L.R. 101 39–05

Emerald Meats (London) Ltd v AIB Group (UK) Plc [2002] EWCA Civ 460 5–03

Emmanuel v Secretary of State for the Home Department [1972] Imm. A.R. 69 57–05

Emokpae v. Chamberlin Solicitors; Webster v Brunel University; Igen Ltd (formerly Leeds Careers Guidance) v Wong; Brunel University v Webster; Chambelin Solicitors v Emokpae. *See* Wong v. Igen Ltd (formerly Leeds Careers Guidance)

Enron (Thrace) Exploration &Production BV v Clapp (No.2) [2005] EWHC 401 49–07

Evans v Secretary of State for the Environment, Transport and the Regions (C63/01) [2005] All E.R. (EC) 763; [2004] R.T.R. 32; [2004] 1 C.M.L.R. 47; [2004] Lloyd's Rep. I.R. 391; *The Times*, December 9, 2003 59–04

Experience Hendrix LLC v PPX Enterprises Inc [2003] EWCA Civ 323; [2003] 1 All E.R. (Comm) 830; [2003] E.M.L.R. 25; [2003] F.S.R. 46; (2003) 26(7) I.P.D. 26046; (2003) 100(22) L.S.G. 29; (2003) 147 S.J.L.B. 509; *The Times*, April 19, 2003, CA (Civ Div); reversing [2002] EWHC 1353; *Daily Telegraph*, July 18, 2002 . . . . 98–07.1

Feldarol Foundry Plc v Hermes Leasing (London) Ltd; Feldarol Foundry Plc v Amari Sant Agata Classics [2004] EWCA Civ 747; (2004) 101(24) L.S.G. 32; (2004) 148 S.J.L.B. 630, CA (Civ Div) 24–01.1

Felix Tena Comadran's Trade Mark No.1567081; IMAGINARIUM Trade Mark. *See* Geoffrey Inc's Trade Mark Application (No.12244)

Fiorentino Comm Giuseppe Srl v Farnesi [2005] EWHC 160; *The Times*, March 3, 2005 6–03

First National Tricity Finance Ltd v Ellis; First National Tricity Finance Ltd v OT Computers Ltd (In Administration); Nagra v OT Computers Ltd. *See* OT Computers Ltd (In Administration), Re

Fladgate Fielder (A Firm) v Smith [2005] All E.R. (D) 264 . . . . 17–09.2

Fletcher v Rylands. *See* Rylands v Fletcher

Foster v Merton and Sutton HA; Thomas v North West Surrey HA; Ikumelo v Newham HA. *See* Naylor v Preston AHA

Fox v United Kingdom (A/182), *sub nom.* Campbell v United Kingdom; Hartley v United Kingdom (1991) 13 E.H.R.R. 157; *The Times*, October 16, 1990; *Guardian*, October 4, 1990 2–03

Friends Provident Life & Pensions Ltd v Sirius International Insurance Corp[2005] EWCA Civ 601; [2005] 2 All E.R. (Comm) 145; [2005] 1 C.L.C. 794; *The Times*, June 8, 2005, CA (Civ Div); affirming [2004] EWHC 1799; [2004] 2 All E.R. (Comm) 707; [2005] Lloyd's Rep. I.R. 135; 2004, (QBD (Comm) 58–10, 60–01

Geoffrey Inc's Trade Mark Application (No.12244), *sub nom.* Felix Tena Comadran's Trade Mark No.1567081; IMAGINARIUM Trade Mark [2004] R.P.C. 30 68–11

Gray v Avadis (No.1) [2003] EWHC 1830; (2003) 100(36) L.S.G. 43; *The Times*, August 19, 2003 28–42

Green v Associated Newspapers Ltd. *See* Greene v Associated Newspapers Ltd

Greene v Associated Newspapers Ltd, *sub nom.* Green v Associated Newspapers Ltd [2004] EWCA Civ 1462; [2005] 1 All E.R. 30; [2005] E.M.L.R. 10; (2004) 101(45) L.S.G. 31; (2004) 148 S.J.L.B. 1318; *The Times*, November 10, 2004; *Independent*, November 9, 2004, CA (Civ Div); affirming [2004] EWHC 2322 . 28–27

TABLE OF CASES

Gregg v Scott [2005] UKHL 2; [2005] 2 W.L.R. 268; (2005) 149 S.J.L.B. 145; *The Times*, January 28, 2005; *Independent*, February 3, 2005, HL; affirming [2002] EWCA Civ 1471; [2003] Lloyd's Rep. Med. 105; (2003) 71 B.M.L.R. 16; (2002) 99(48) L.S.G. 27; (2002) 99(49) L.S.G. 19; (2002) 146 S.J.L.B. 247; *The Times*, November 4, 2002 .... 72–04.1, 75–04

Hanning v Top Deck Travel Group Ltd (1994) 68 P. & C.R. 14 83–03

Harbottle (Mercantile) Ltd v National Westminster Bank Ltd. *See* RD Harbottle (Mercantile) Ltd v National Westminster Bank Ltd

Harrison v Teton Valley Trading Co Ltd, *sub nom.* CHINAWHITE Trade Mark; Harrison's Trade Mark Application [2004] EWCA Civ 1028; [2004] 1 W.L.R. 2577; [2005] F.S.R. 10; (2004) 27(8) I.P.D. 4; (2004) 148 S.J.L.B. 1061; *The Times*, August 19, 2004, CA (Civ Div); affirming [2002] EWHC 3009; [2004] F.S.R. 13 68–10

Harrow LBC v Quazi; Harrow LBC v Qazi. *See* Qazi v Harrow LBC

Hill v Chief Constable of West Yorkshire [1989] A.C. 53; [1988] 2 W.L.R. 1049; [1988] 2 All E.R. 238; 152 L.G.R. 709; (1988) 152 L.G. Rev 709; (1988) 85(20) L.S.G. 34; (1988) 138 N.L.J. Rep. 126; (1988) 132 S.J. 700, HL; affirming [1988] Q.B. 60; [1987] 2 W.L.R. 1126; [1987] 1 All E.R. 1173; 151 L.G.R. 729; (1987) 151 L.G. Rev 729; (1987) 84 L.S.G. 982; (1987) 137 N.L.J. 222; (1987) 131 S.J. 626, CA (Civ Div); affirming (1986) 136 N.L.J. 238 .... 2–06B

Hinton v University of East London [2005] EWCA Civ 532; [2005] I.C.R. 1260; [2005] I.R.L.R. 552, CA (Civ Div) 31–03.5

Holme v Brunskill (1877) 3 Q.B.D. 494 11–15

Hotson v East Berkshire HA, *sub nom.* Hotson v Fitzgerald [1987] A.C. 750; [1987] 3 W.L.R. 232; [1987] 2 All E.R. 909; [1955-95] P.N.L.R. 330; (1987) 84 L.S.G. 2365; (1987) 131 S.J. 975, HL; reversing [1987] 2 W.L.R. 287; [1987] 1 All E.R. 210; (1987) 84 L.S.G. 37; (1986) 136 N.L.J. 1163; (1986) 130 S.J. 925, CA (Civ Div); affirming [1985] 1 W.L.R. 1036; [1985] 3 All E.R. 167; (1985) 82 L.S.G. 2818; (1985) 129 S.J. 558 .... 72–04.1

—— v Fitzgerald. *See* Hotson v East Berkshire HA

Huang v Secretary of State for the Home Department, *sub nom.* Abu-Qulbain v Secretary of State for the Home Department; Kashmiri v Secretary of State for the Home Department [2005] EWCA Civ 105; (2005) 149 S.J.L.B. 297; *The Times*, March 16, 2005 57–04

Hughes v Riley [2005] EWCA Civ 1129, CA (Civ Div) 38–03

Humphreys v Humphreys [2004] EWHC 2201; [2005] 1 F.C.R. 712; [2004] W.T.L.R. 1425 17–05

Hunter v Canary Wharf Ltd, *sub nom.* Hunter v London Docklands Development Corp [1997] A.C. 655; [1997] 2 W.L.R. 684; [1998] 1 W.L.R. 434; [1997] 2 All E.R. 426; [1997] C.L.C. 1045; 84 B.L.R. 1; 54 Con. L.R. 12; [1997] Env L.R. 488; [1997] 2 F.L.R. 342; (1998) 30 H.L.R. 409; [1997] Fam. Law 601; [1997] E.G.C.S. 59; (1997) 94(19) L.S.G. 25; (1997) 147 N.L.J. 634; (1997) 141 S.J.L.B. 108; [1997] N.P.C. 64; *The Times*, April 25, 1997; *Independent*, May 2, 1997, HL; affirming [1996] 2 W.L.R. 348; [1996] 1 All E.R. 482; [1996] C.L.C. 197; 75 B.L.R. 27; 47 Con. L.R. 136; [1996] Env L.R. 138; (1996) 28 H.L.R. 383; [1995] E.G.C.S. 153; (1995) 92(39) L.S.G. 28; (1995) 145 N.L.J. 1645; (1995) 139 S.J.L.B. 214; [1995] N.P.C. 155; *The Times*, October 13, 1995; *Independent*, October 19, 1995, CA (Civ Div); affirming in part *Independent*, December 20, 1994; *Independent*, January 23, 1995 (C.S.) 38–14.1

—— v London Docklands Development Corp. *See* Hunter v Canary Wharf Ltd

Jameel v Wall Street Journal Europe SPRL (No.3) [2005] EWCA Civ 74; (2005) 102(15) L.S.G. 33; *The Times*, February 14, 2005; *Independent*, February 9, 2005, CA (Civ Div); affirming [2004] EWHC 37; [2004] E.M.L.R. 11 .... 28–44, 28–56

Jobling v Associated Dairies [1982] A.C. 794; [1981] 3 W.L.R. 155; [1981] 2 All E.R. 752; 125 S.J. 481, HL; affirming [1981] Q.B. 389; [1980] 3 W.L.R. 704; [1980] 3 All E.R. 769; 124 S.J. 631 72–06

Jones v Commerzbank AG, *sub nom.* Commerzbank AG v Jones; Commerzbank AG v Price-Jones; Price-Jones v Commerzbank AG [2003] EWCA Civ 1663; (2003) 147 S.J.L.B. 1397; [2004] 1 P. & C.R. DG15; *The Times*, November 26, 2003; *Independent*, December 4, 2003, CA (Civ Div); reversing 5–11.1

TABLE OF CASES

Joseph v City of London Real Property Co Ltd. *See* Midtown Ltd v City of London Real Property Co Ltd

Keegan v Chief Constable of Merseyside [2003] EWCA Civ 936; [2003] 1 W.L.R. 2187; (2003) 100(34) L.S.G. 32; (2003) 147 S.J.L.B. 869; *The Times*, July 17, 2003 .... 2–06A

Keeley v Pashen [2004] EWCA Civ 1491; [2005] 1 W.L.R. 1226; [2005] R.T.R. 10; [2005] Lloyd's Rep. I.R. 289; (2004) 101(45) L.S.G. 32; *The Times*, November 17, 2004 59–02

Khatun v United Kingdom (38387/97) (1998) 26 E.H.R.R. CD212, Eur Comm HR ... 38–12

King v Lewis [2004] EWCA Civ 1329; [2005] E.M.L.R. 4; (2004) 148 S.J.L.B. 1248; *The Times*, October 26, 2004; *Independent*, November 11, 2004, CA (Civ Div); affirming [2004] EWHC 168; [2004] I.L.Pr. 31 28–21

Kirin-Amgen Inc v Transkaryotic Therapies Inc (No.2), *sub nom.* Kirin-Amgen Inc's European Patent (No.148605) (No.2); Kirin-Amgen Inc v Hoechst Marion Roussel Ltd (No.2) [2004] UKHL 46; [2005] 1 All E.R. 667; [2005] R.P.C. 9; (2004) 148 S.J.L.B. 1249, HL; affirming [2002] EWCA Civ 1096; [2003] E.N.P.R. 4; [2003] R.P.C. 3; (2002) 25(11) I.P.D. 25076, CA (Civ Div); reversing in part [2002] R.P.C. 2; (2001) 24(8) I.P.D. 24051; (2001) 98(24) L.S.G. 45; *The Times*, June 1, 2001 64–02

Kirin-Amgen Inc's European Patent (No.148605) (No.2); Kirin-Amgen Inc v Hoechst Marion Roussel Ltd (No.2). *See* Kirin-Amgen Inc v Transkaryotic Therapies Inc (No.2)

Kumar v Commissioner of Police of the Metropolis, unreported, January 31, 1995 ... 2–06B

Kuwait Oil Tanker Co SAK v Al-Bader (No.3) [2000] 2 All E.R. (Comm) 271; (2000) 97(23) L.S.G. 44; *The Times*, May 30, 2000; *Independent*, June 26, 2000 (C.S.), CA (Civ Div); affirming *Independent*, January 11, 1999 (C.S.) 50–02

Kvaerner John Brown Ltd v Midland Bank Plc [1998] C.L.C. 446 8–05

LTJ Diffusion SA v Sadas Vertbaudet SA (C291/00) [2003] E.C.R. I-2799; [2003] C.E.C. 283; [2003] E.T.M.R. 83; [2003] F.S.R. 34; *The Times*, March 26, 2003 [2002] E.T.M.R. 40; [2003] F.S.R. 1 .... 68–01.1

La Mer Technology Inc v Laboratoires Goemar SA (C259/02), *sub nom.* Laboratories Goemar SA's Trade Marks Nos.1338514 and 1402537 [2004] E.T.M.R. 47; [2004] F.S.R. 38 68–11

Laiqat v Majid [2005] EWHC 1305; [2005] 26 E.G.C.S. 130; [2005] N.P.C. 81, QBD . 40–01

Lambretta Clothing Co Ltd v Next Retail Plc. *See* Lambretta Clothing Co Ltd v Teddy Smith (UK) Ltd

—— v Teddy Smith (UK) Ltd, *sub nom.* Lambretta Clothing Co Ltd v Next Retail Plc [2004] EWCA Civ 886; [2005] R.P.C. 6; (2004) 148 S.J.L.B. 911; *The Times*, September 28, 2004, CA (Civ Div); affirming [2003] EWHC 1204; [2003] R.P.C. 41 .... 66–03, 67–02

Libertel Groep BV v Benelux Merkenbureau (C104/01) [2004] Ch. 83; [2004] 2 W.L.R. 1081; [2003] E.C.R. I-3793; [2003] E.T.M.R. 63; [2004] F.S.R. 4; *The Times*, May 12, 2003 [2003] E.T.M.R. 41 68–10

Light v Ty Europe Ltd [2003] EWCA Civ 1238; [2004] 1 Lloyd's Rep. 693; [2004] 1 C.L.C. 71; [2004] E.C.C. 39; [2003] Eu. L.R. 858; (2003) 100(38) L.S.G. 33; *The Times*, August 21, 2003, CA (Civ Div); reversing [2003] EWHC 174; [2003] 1 All E.R. (Comm) 568; [2003] Eu. L.R. 268 .... 20–01.2

Lister v Hesley Hall Ltd [2001] UKHL 22; [2002] 1 A.C. 215; [2001] 2 W.L.R. 1311; [2001] 2 All E.R. 769; [2001] I.C.R. 665; [2001] I.R.L.R. 472; [2001] Emp. L.R. 819; [2001] 2 F.L.R. 307; [2001] 2 F.C.R. 97; (2001) 3 L.G.L.R. 49; [2001] E.L.R. 422; [2001] Fam. Law 595; (2001) 98(24) L.S.G. 45; (2001) 151 N.L.J. 728; (2001) 145 S.J.L.B. 126; [2001] N.P.C. 89; *The Times*, May 10, 2001; *Independent*, June 11, 2001 (C.S.); *Daily Telegraph*, May 8, 2001, HL; reversing *The Times*, October 13, 1999; *Independent*, November 22, 1999 (C.S.) 2–01

—— v Stubbs (1890) L.R. 45 52–04

Lloyds TSB Bank Plc v Hayward [2005] EWCA Civ 466, CA (Civ Div); affirming [2004] EWHC 1798 11–15

Loftus-Brigham v Ealing LBC [2003] EWCA Civ 1490; (2004) 20 Const. L.J. 82 38–09

TABLE OF CASES

Lonrho Ltd v Shell Petroleum Co Ltd (No.2) [1982] A.C. 173; [1981] 3 W.L.R. 33; [1981] 2 All E.R. 456; 125 S.J. 429, HL; affirming [1981] Com. L.R. 74; 125 S.J. 255, CA (Civ Div); affirming [1981] Com. L.R. 6; *The Times*, December 2, 1980	50–03
Lonrho Plc v Al-Fayed (No.1) [1992] 1 A.C. 448; [1991] 3 W.L.R. 188; [1991] 3 All E.R. 303; [1991] B.C.C. 641; [1991] B.C.L.C. 779; (1991) 141 N.L.J. 927; (1991) 135 S.J.L.B. 68; *The Times*, July 3, 1991; *Independent*, July 3, 1991; *Financial Times*, July 3, 1991; *Guardian*, June 28, 1991, HL; affirming [1990] 2 Q.B. 479; [1989] 3 W.L.R. 631; [1989] 2 All E.R. 65; [1989] B.C.L.C. 485; [1989] P.C.C. 215; (1989) 139 N.L.J. 539, CA (Civ Div); reversing [1990] 1 Q.B. 490; [1989] 2 W.L.R. 356; (1988) 4 B.C.C. 688; [1989] B.C.L.C. 75; [1989] P.C.C. 173; (1989) 86(10) L.S.G. 43; (1988) 138 N.L.J. Rep. 225; (1989) 133 S.J. 220; *Independent*, July 19, 1988	50–03
Lordsvale Finance Plc v Bank of Zambia [1996] Q.B. 752; [1996] 3 W.L.R. 688; [1996] 3 All E.R. 156; [1996] C.L.C. 1849; *The Times*, April 8, 1996	5–03
Lumbermen Mutual Casualty Co v Bovis Lend Lease Ltd (Preliminary Issues). *See* Lumbermens Mutual Casualty Co v Bovis Lend Lease Ltd (Preliminary Issues)	
Lumbermens Mutual Casualty Co v ——, *sub nom.* Lumbermen Mutual Casualty Co v Bovis Lend Lease Ltd (Preliminary Issues) [2004] EWHC 2197; [2005] B.L.R. 47; [2005] Lloyd's Rep. I.R. 74; [2004] 42 E.G.C.S. 160	58–15
M v Calderdale and Kirklees HA (formerly West Yorkshire HA) [1998] Lloyd's Rep. Med. 157	72–04.1
Macklin v Dowsett [2004] EWCA Civ 904; [2004] 2 E.G.L.R. 75; [2004] 34 E.G. 68; [2004] 26 E.G.C.S. 193	17–04
Majorowski v Guy's and St Thomas's NHS Trust. *See* Majrowski v Guy's and St Thomas's NHS Trust	
Majrowski v ——, *sub nom.* Majrowski v Guy's and St Thomas's NHS Trust [2005] EWCA Civ 251; (2005) 149 S.J.L.B. 358; *The Times*, March 21, 2005; *Independent*, April 8, 2005	54–02.2, 71–07
Mandrake Holdings Ltd v Countrywide Assured Group Plc [2005] EWCA Civ 840, CA (Civ Div); affirming [2005] EWHC 311, Ch D	58–13
Marcic v Thames Water Utilities Ltd, *sub nom.* Thames Water Utilities Ltd v Marcic [2003] UKHL 66; [2004] 2 A.C. 42; [2003] 3 W.L.R. 1603; [2004] 1 All E.R. 135; [2004] B.L.R. 1; 91 Con. L.R. 1; [2004] Env L.R. 25; [2004] H.R.L.R. 10; [2004] U.K.H.R.R. 253; [2003] 50 E.G.C.S. 95; (2004) 101(4) L.S.G. 32; (2003) 153 N.L.J. 1869; (2003) 147 S.J.L.B. 1429; [2003] N.P.C. 150; *The Times*, December 5, 2003; *Independent*, December 9, 2003, HL; reversing [2002] EWCA Civ 64; [2002] Q.B. 929; [2002] 2 W.L.R. 932; [2002] 2 All E.R. 55; [2002] B.L.R. 174; [2002] T.C.L.R. 15; 81 Con. L.R. 193; [2002] Env L.R. 32; [2003] E.H.L.R. 2; [2002] H.R.L.R. 22; [2002] U.K.H.R.R. 1041; (2002) 18 Const. L.J. 152; [2002] 7 E.G.C.S. 122; (2002) 99(12) L.S.G. 34; (2002) 146 S.J.L.B. 51; [2002] N.P.C. 20; *The Times*, February 14, 2002; *Independent*, February 12, 2002, CA (Civ Div); reversing in part [2001] 3 All E.R. 698; (2001) 3 T.C.L.R. 28; 77 Con. L.R. 42; [2002] Env L.R. 6; [2001] H.R.L.R. 52; [2001] 3 E.G.L.R. 111; [2001] N.P.C. 95; [2001] E.H.L.R. Dig. 6; *Independent*, July 9, 2001 (C.S.)	38–02, 38–05—38–06
Mattos Junior v MacDaniels Ltd; Barros Mattos Junior v General Securities & Finance Co Ltd. *See* Barros Mattos Junior v MacDaniels Ltd	
McBrearty v Ministry of Defence. *See* Elguzouli-Daf v Commissioner of Police of the Metropolis	
Mercer v Chief Constable of Lancashire, *sub nom.* Holder v Chief Constable of Lancashire [1991] 1 W.L.R. 367; [1991] 2 All E.R. 504; *The Times*, February 22, 1991; *Independent*, March 6, 1991	2–03
Midco Holdings v Piper [2004] EWCA Civ 476; [2004] N.P.C. 59	49–05
Midtown Ltd v City of London Real Property Co Ltd, *sub nom.* Joseph v City of London Real Property Co Ltd [2005] EWHC 33; [2005] 14 E.G. 130; [2005] 4 E.G.C.S. 166; (2005) 102(14) L.S.G. 26; [2005] N.P.C. 13; *The Times*, February 14, 2005	38–10

Table of Cases

Milne v Express Newspapers Ltd (No.1) [2004] EWCA Civ 664; [2005] 1 W.L.R. 772; [2005] 1 All E.R. 1021; [2004] E.M.L.R. 24; (2004) 148 S.J.L.B. 696; *Independent*, June 11, 2004, CA (Civ Div); affirming [2002] EWHC 2564; [2003] 1 W.L.R. 927; [2003] 1 All E.R. 482; [2003] E.M.L.R. 22; (2003) 100(5) L.S.G. 32; *The Times*, December 9, 2002 .... 28–57A

Mistry v Thakor [2005] EWCA Civ 953, CA (Civ Div) 38–17

Moroak v Cromie, UKEAT/0093/05/DM, EAT 31–03.1

Morris v Jones [2002] EWCA Civ 1790 49–02

Murray Clayton v Rafidair Bank. *See* United Trading Corp SA v Allied Arab Bank

N (A Child) v Entry Clearance Officer. *See* N (A Child) v Immigration Appeal Tribunal

——— v Immigration Appeal Tribunal, *sub nom.* N (A Child) v Entry Clearance Officer [2001] I.N.L.R. 26; (2000) 97(36) L.S.G. 41; *The Times*, September 6, 2000, CA (Civ Div)... 57–05

Nail v Jones. *See* Nail v News Group Newspapers Ltd

——— v News Group Newspapers Ltd, *sub nom.* Nail v Jones [2004] EWCA Civ 1708; [2005] 1 All E.R. 1040; [2005] E.M.L.R. 12; (2005) 155 N.L.J. 111; *The Times*, January 6, 2005; *Independent*, January 14, 2005, CA (Civ Div); affirming [2004] EWHC 647; [2004] E.M.L.R. 20 28–48

National Basketball Association v Athletic Union of Constantinople (AEK) (Application to Strike Out); Athletic Union of Constantinople v National Basketball Association (No.2). *See* Athletic Union of Constantinople (AEK) v National Basketball Association (Application to Strike Out)

National Westminster Bank Plc v Bowles [2005] EWHC 182 11–12

——— v Somer International (UK) Ltd [2001] EWCA Civ 970; [2002] Q.B. 1286; [2002] 3 W.L.R. 64; [2002] 1 All E.R. 198; [2001] Lloyd's Rep. Bank. 263; [2001] C.L.C. 1579; *Independent*, June 26, 2001 98–08

Naylor v Preston AHA, *sub nom.* Foster v Merton and Sutton HA; Thomas v North West Surrey HA; Ikumelo v Newham HA [1987] 1 W.L.R. 958; [1987] 2 All E.R. 353; (1987) 84 L.S.G. 1494; (1987) 137 N.L.J. 474; (1987) 131 S.J. 596 72–06

Network Rail Infrastructure Ltd v Morris (t/a Soundstar Studio) [2004] EWCA Civ 172; [2004] Env L.R. 41; (2004) 148 S.J.L.B. 266................. 38–04—38–05, 38–08

Niersmans v Pesticcio *See* Pesticcio v Huet

Nigel Upchurch Associates v Aldridge Estates Investment Co [1993] 1 Lloyd's Rep. 535 58–14

Niru Battery Manufacturing Co v Milestone Trading Ltd (No.1) [2003] EWCA Civ 1446; [2004] Q.B. 985; [2004] 2 W.L.R. 1415; [2004] 1 All E.R. (Comm) 193; [2004] 1 Lloyd's Rep. 344; [2004] 1 C.L.C. 647; [2004] W.T.L.R. 377; (2003) 100(44) L.S.G. 33; *The Times*, October 30, 2003, CA (Civ Div); affirming [2002] EWHC 1425; [2002] 2 All E.R. (Comm) 705..................... 5–12.1, 98–08

OT Computers Ltd (In Administration), Re, *sub nom.* First National Tricity Finance Ltd v Ellis; First National Tricity Finance Ltd v OT Computers Ltd (In Administration); Nagra v OT Computers Ltd [2004] EWCA Civ 653; [2004] Ch. 317; [2004] 3 W.L.R. 886; [2004] 2 All E.R. (Comm) 331; [2004] 2 B.C.L.C. 682; [2004] 2 C.L.C. 863; [2004] B.P.I.R. 932; [2004] Lloyd's Rep. I.R. 669; *The Times*, May 31, 2004, CA (Civ Div); reversing [2003] EWHC 2490; [2004] 1 All E.R. (Comm) 320; [2004] B.P.I.R. 195 58–14

Office for Harmonisation in the Internal Market (Trade Marks and Designs) (OHIM) v Wm Wrigley Jr Co (C191/01 P), *sub nom.* Wm Wrigley Jr Co v Office for Harmonisation in the Internal Market (Trade Marks and Designs) (OHIM) [2004] 1 W.L.R. 1728; [2004] All E.R. (EC) 1040; [2004] E.T.M.R. 9; [2004] R.P.C. 18; *The Times*, November 10, 2003, ECJ; reversing [2003] E.T.M.R. 88; (2003) 26(8) I.P.D. 26049 68–10

Olympic Airways v Husain, 124 SCt 1221 (2004) 4–06

Paul v Chief Constable of Humberside [2004] EWCA Civ 308, CA (Civ Div) 2–05.2

Pearce v United Bristol Healthcare NHS Trust [1999] E.C.C. 167; [1999] P.I.Q.R. P53; (1999) 48 B.M.L.R. 118.. 72–04.1

Peregrine Systems Ltd v Steria Ltd [2005] EWCA Civ 239, CA (Civ Div); affirming [2004] EWHC 275; [2004] Masons C.L.R. 20......................... 27–05, 27–11

TABLE OF CASES

Pesticcio v Huet, sub nom. Niersmans v Pesticcio [2004] EWCA Civ 372; [2004] W.T.L.R. 699; (2004) 154 N.L.J. 653; (2004) 148 S.J.L.B. 420; [2004] N.P.C. 55; *Independent*, April 7, 2004, CA (Civ Div); affirming [2003] EWHC 2293; (2003) 73 B.M.L.R. 57; [2003] W.T.L.R. 1327; [2003] 2 P. & C.R. DG8 17–05

Pickett v Motor Insurers Bureau. *See* Pickett v Roberts

—— v Roberts, sub nom. Pickett v Motor Insurers Bureau [2004] EWCA Civ 6; [2004] 1 W.L.R. 2450; [2004] 2 All E.R. 685; [2004] R.T.R. 28; [2004] Lloyd's Rep. I.R. 513; [2004] P.I.Q.R. P24; (2004) 148 S.J.L.B. 117 59–04

Polly Peck International Plc v Nadir (Asil) (No.2) [1992] 4 All E.R. 769; [1992] 2 Lloyd's Rep 238; [1993] B.C.L.C. 187; (1992) 142 N.L.J. 671; *The Times*, March 24, 1992; *Independent*, March 20, 1992; *Financial Times*, March 27, 1992 .... 5–12.1

Potter v UNISON, unreported, March 1, 2004, EAT 34–08

Qazi v Harrow LBC, *sub nom.* Harrow LBC v Quazi; Harrow LBC v Qazi [2003] UKHL 43; [2004] 1 A.C. 983; [2003] 3 W.L.R. 792; [2003] 4 All E.R. 461; [2003] 2 F.L.R. 973; [2003] 3 F.C.R. 43; [2003] H.R.L.R. 40; [2003] U.K.H.R.R. 974; [2003] H.L.R. 75; [2004] 1 P. & C.R. 19; [2004] L. & T.R. 9; [2003] 3 E.G.L.R. 109; [2003] Fam. Law 875; (2003) 100(38) L.S.G. 34; (2003) 147 S.J.L.B. 937; [2003] N.P.C. 101; *The Times*, August 1, 2003; *Independent*, October 3, 2003, HL; reversing [2001] EWCA Civ 1834; [2002] U.K.H.R.R. 316; [2002] H.L.R. 14; [2002] L. & T.R. 23; *Independent*, January 14, 2002 (C.S.) 38–01, 38–12

R (A Minor) (No.2), Re. *See* Robertson v Nottingham HA

RD Harbottle (Mercantile) Ltd v National Westminster Bank Ltd, *sub nom.* Harbottle (Mercantile) Ltd v National Westminster Bank Ltd [1978] Q.B. 146; [1977] 3 W.L.R. 752; [1977] 2 All E.R. 862; 121 S.J. 745 8–05

R. (on the application of Bagdanavicius) v Secretary of State for the Home Department [2005] UKHL 38; [2005] 2 W.L.R. 1359; [2005] 4 All E.R. 263; [2005] H.R.L.R. 24; [2005] I.N.L.R. 422; *The Times*, May 30, 2005; *Independent*, June 15, 2005, HL; affirming [2003] EWCA Civ 1605; [2004] 1 W.L.R. 1207; [2004] Imm. A.R. 36; [2004] I.N.L.R. 163; [2004] A.C.D. 6; (2004) 101(2) L.S.G. 29; *The Times*, November 21, 2003; *Independent*, November 21, 2003, CA (Civ Div); affirming [2003] EWHC 854 57–04

—— (on the application of Laporte) v Chief Constable of Gloucestershire [2004] EWCA Civ 1639; [2005] 2 W.L.R. 789; [2005] 1 All E.R. 473; (2005) 102(6) L.S.G. 32; *The Times*, December 13, 2004; *Independent*, December 14, 2004, CA (Civ Div); affirming [2004] EWHC 253; [2004] 2 All E.R. 874; [2004] U.K.H.R.R. 484; [2004] A.C.D. 34; (2004) 154 N.L.J. 308; *The Times*, February 26, 2004 2–03

—— (on the application of Marper) v Chief Constable of South Yorkshire. *See* R. (on the application of S) v Chief Constable of South Yorkshire

—— (on the application of Ratnam) v Secretary of State for the Home Department [2003] EWHC 398 57–06

—— (on the application of S) v Chief Constable of South Yorkshire, *sub nom.* R. (on the application of Marper) v Chief Constable of South Yorkshire [2004] UKHL 39; [2004] 1 W.L.R. 2196; [2004] 4 All E.R. 193; [2004] H.R.L.R. 35; [2004] U.K.H.R.R. 967; [2005] Crim. L.R. 136; (2004) 101(34) L.S.G. 29; (2004) 154 N.L.J. 1183; (2004) 148 S.J.L.B. 914; *The Times*, July 23, 2004; *Independent*, July 29, 2004, HL; affirming [2002] EWCA Civ 1275; [2002] 1 W.L.R. 3223; [2003] 1 All E.R. 148; [2003] 1 Cr. App. R. 16; [2003] H.R.L.R. 1; 13 B.H.R.C. 569; [2003] Crim. L.R. 39; [2003] A.C.D. 8; (2002) 99(40) L.S.G. 32; (2002) 152 N.L.J. 1483; (2002) 146 S.J.L.B. 207; *The Times*, October 3, 2002;*Independent*, October 1, 2002, CA (Civ Div); affirming [2002] EWHC 478; *The Times*, April 4, 2002; *Daily Telegraph*, April 11, 2002 2–01

R. v Immigration Appeal Tribunal Ex p. Mahmood (Sajid) [1988] Imm. A.R. 121 57–05

—— v Immigration Appeal Tribunal Ex p. Uddin (Fojor) and Uddin (Nur) [1986] Imm. A.R. 203 57–05

—— v Secretary of State for the Home Department Ex p. Boybeyi [1997] Imm. A.R. 491; [1997] I.N.L.R. 130; [1997] C.O.D. 455; (1997) 94(23) L.S.G. 27; (1997) 141 S.J.L.B. 130; *The Times*, June 5, 1997, CA (Civ Div) 57–06

Rackham v Sandy [2005] EWHC 482 28–55

Radio Taxicabs (London) Ltd (t/a Radio Taxis) v Owner Drivers Radio Taxi Services Ltd (t/a Dial-a-Cab) [2004] R.P.C. 19; [2002] Masons C.L.R. 29 69–02

TABLE OF CASES

Ramos *v* Immigration Appeal Tribunal [1989] Imm. A.R. 148 57–05
Reed Executive Plc *v* Reed Business Information Ltd [2004] EWCA Civ 159; [2004] E.T.M.R. 56; [2004] Info. T.L.R. 55; [2004] R.P.C. 40; [2004] Masons C.L.R. 29; (2004) 27(6) I.P.D. 27058; (2004) 148 S.J.L.B. 298; *The Times*, March 9, 2004, CA (Civ Div); reversing [2002] EWHC 1015; [2003] Info. T.L.R. 7; [2003] R.P.C. 12; [2002] Masons C.L.R. 40; (2002) 99(29) L.S.G. 33; (2002) 146 S.J.L.B. 151; [2003] E.T.M.R. CN7; *The Times*, June 13, 2002 .... 68–01.1, 69–10
Research in Motion UK Ltd *v* (1) Impro Licensing S.A.R.L. (2) Lextron Systems, Inc [2004] EWHC 1292 (Pat) 64–12.1
Re-Source America International Ltd *v* Platt Site Services Ltd[2004] EWCA Civ 665; 95 Con. L.R. 1; [2004] N.P.C. 89, CA (Civ Div); affirming [2003] EWHC 1142; 90 Con. L.R. 139, QBD (TCC) 38–01
Robertson *v* Nottingham HA, *sub nom.* R (A Minor) (No.2), Re [1997] 8 Med. L.R. 1; (1997) 33 B.M.L.R. 178, CA (Civ Div); affirming [1996] 7 Med. L.R. 421 .... 72–04.1
Royal Products *v* Midland Bank [1981] 2 Lloyd's Rep. 194; [1981] Com. L.R. 93 5–06
Rylands *v* Fletcher, *sub nom.* Fletcher *v* Rylands (1868) L.R. 3 H.L. 330, HL; affirming (1865-66) L.R. 1 Ex. 265; [1865–66] All E.R. Rep. 1; (1866) 4 Hurl. & C. 263, Ex Chamber; reversing (1865) 3 Hurl. & C. 774 .... 38–02, 38–05, 38–12
SAM Business Systems Ltd *v* Hedley & Co [2002] EWHC 2733 .... 27–04, 27–07
Sawkins *v* Hyperion Records Ltd [2004] EWHC 1530; [2004] 4 All E.R. 418; [2005] E.C.D.R. 10; [2004] E.M.L.R. 27; [2005] R.P.C. 4; (2004) 101(35) L.S.G. 35; *The Times*, July 26, 2004 66–03
Sayers *v* SmithKline Beecham Plc [2005] EWHC 539 37–02
Scottish Equitable Plc *v* Thompson [2003] EWCA Civ 225; [2003] H.L.R. 48; [2003] 7 E.G.C.S. 137 13–05
Secretary of State for the Environment, Food and Rural Affairs *v* Drury. *See* Drury *v* Secretary of State for the Environment, Food and Rural Affairs
Shield Mark BV *v* Kist (t/a Memex) (C283/01) [2004] Ch. 97; [2004] 2 W.L.R. 1117; [2004] All E.R. (EC) 277; [2005] 1 C.M.L.R. 41; [2004] C.E.C. 228; [2004] E.T.M.R. 33; [2004] R.P.C. 17; *The Times*, December 4, 2003 [2003] E.T.M.R. 64 68–10
Sidaway *v* Board of Governors of the Bethlem Royal Hospital [1985] A.C. 871; [1985] 2 W.L.R. 480; [1985] 1 All E.R. 643; (1985) 82 L.S.G. 1256; (1985) 135 N.L.J. 203; (1985) 129 S.J. 154, HL; affirming [1984] Q.B. 493; [1984] 2 W.L.R. 778; [1984] 1 All E.R. 1018; (1984) 81 L.S.G. 899; (1984) 128 S.J. 301 .... 72–04.1
Sinclair Investment Holdings SA *v* Versailles Trade Finance Ltd [2004] EWHC 2169, Ch D 53–07.1
Sir Robert McAlpine Ltd *v* Alfred McAlpine Plc [2004] EWHC 630, [2004] R.P.C. 36; (2004) 27(7) I.P.D. 27071 .... 69–02, 69–07
Sloley *v* Entry Clearance Officer [1973] Imm.A.R. 54 57–05
Southwark LBC *v* Mills, *sub nom.* Baxter *v* Camden LBC (No.2); Southwark LBC *v* Tanner [2001] 1 A.C. 1; [1999] 3 W.L.R. 939; [1999] 4 All E.R. 449; [2000] Env L.R. 112; (2000) 32 H.L.R. 148; [2000] B.L.G.R. 138; [2000] L. & T.R. 159; [1999] 3 E.G.L.R. 35; [1999] 45 E.G. 179; [1999] E.G.C.S. 122; (1999) 96(42) L.S.G. 45; (1999) 96(42) L.S.G. 41; (1999) 149 N.L.J. 1618; (1999) 143 S.J.L.B. 249; [1999] N.P.C. 123; (2000) 79 P. & C.R. D13; *The Times*, October 22, 1999 , HL; affirming [2001] Ch. 1; [1999] 2 W.L.R. 409; (1999) 31 H.L.R. 187; [1999] B.L.G.R. 71; (1998) 10 Admin. L.R. 621; [1998] L. & T.R. 251; [1998] 3 E.G.L.R. 46; [1998] 45 E.G. 151; (1998) 162 J.P.N. 945; [1998] E.G.C.S. 132; (1998) 95(34) L.S.G. 31; (1998) 142 S.J.L.B. 221; [1998] N.P.C. 126; *The Times*, August 20, 1998; *Independent*, October 2, 1998, CA (Civ Div); reversing [1998] 3 W.L.R. 49; (1998) 10 Admin. L.R. 353; [1998] 2 E.G.L.R. 30; [1998] 22 E.G. 151; (1998) 162 J.P.N. 722; [1998] E.G.C.S. 39; (1998) 95(16) L.S.G. 25; (1998) 142 S.J.L.B. 119; [1998] N.P.C. 34; *The Times*, March 11, 1998 86–05
State Trading Corp of India Ltd *v* ED & F Man (Sugar) Ltd [1981] Com. L.R. 235 ... 8–05
Stockport MBC *v* Reddish Vale Golf Club; Stockport MBC *v* British Gas Plc; British Gas Plc *v* Stockport MBC. *See* Transco Plc *v* Stockport MBC
Sutton *v* Mishcon de Reya [2003] EWHC 3166; [2004] 1 F.L.R. 837; [2004] 3 F.C.R. 142; [2004] Fam. Law 247; *The Times*, January 28, 2004 17–03

Table of Cases

T (formerly H) v Nugent Care Society (formerly Catholic Social Services) [2004] EWCA Civ 51; [2004] 1 W.L.R. 1129; [2004] 3 All E.R. 671; (2004) 101(6) L.S.G. 33; (2004) 148 S.J.L.B. 114; *The Times*, January 28, 2004; *Independent*, January 22, 2004 37–02

T & N Ltd (In Administration) v Royal & Sun Alliance Plc [2003] EWHC 1016; [2003] 2 All E.R. (Comm) 939; [2004] Lloyd's Rep. I.R. 106; (2003) 153 N.L.J. 750, Ch D 58–14

Tahir v Haringey HA [1998] Lloyd's Rep. Med. 104 .... 72–04.1

Tarbuck v Avon Insurance Plc [2002] Q.B. 571; [2001] 3 W.L.R. 1502; [2001] 2 All E.R. 503; [2001] 1 All E.R. (Comm) 422; [2001] B.P.I.R. 1142; [2002] Lloyd's Rep. I.R. 393; (2001) 151 N.L.J. 18 58–14

Taylor v Chief Constable of Thames Valley [2004] EWCA Civ 858; [2004] 1 W.L.R. 3155; [2004] 3 All E.R. 503; (2004) 101(32) L.S.G. 36; (2004) 148 S.J.L.B. 877; *The Times*, July 13, 2004 2–03

Thake v Maurice [1986] Q.B. 644; [1986] 2 W.L.R. 337; [1986] 1 All E.R. 479; (1986) 83 L.S.G. 123; (1986) 136 N.L.J. 92, CA (Civ Div); affirming [1985] 2 W.L.R. 215; [1984] 2 All E.R. 513; (1985) 82 L.S.G. 871; (1985) 129 S.J. 86 .... 72–04.1

Thames Water Utilities Ltd v Marcic. *See* Marcic v Thames Water Utilities Ltd

Themehelp Ltd v West [1996] Q.B. 84; [1995] 3 W.L.R. 751; [1995] 4 All E.R. 215; *The Times*, May 2, 1995; *Independent*, June 26, 1995 (C.S.) 8–05

Thomas Cook (New Zealand) Ltd v Inland Revenue Commissioner [2004] UKPC 53; [2005] S.T.C. 297; [2004] S.T.I. 2378, PC; affirming [2003] 2 N.Z.L.R. 296 .. 9–01.2

Trade Indemnity Co Ltd v Workington Harbour and Dock Board (No.1), *sub nom.* Workington Harbour and Dock Board v Trade Indemnity Co Ltd [1937] A.C. 1; (1936) 54 Ll. L. Rep. 103, HL; affirming (1934) 49 Ll. L. Rep. 430, CA; reversing (1933) 47 Ll. L. Rep. 305 11–15

Transco Plc v Stockport MBC, *sub nom.* Stockport MBC v Reddish Vale Golf Club; Stockport MBC v British Gas Plc; British Gas Plc v Stockport MBC [2003] UKHL 61; [2004] 2 A.C. 1; [2003] 3 W.L.R. 1467; [2004] 1 All E.R. 589; 91 Con. L.R. 28; [2004] Env L.R. 24; [2003] 48 E.G.C.S. 127; (2003) 153 N.L.J. 1791; (2003) 147 S.J.L.B. 1367; [2003] N.P.C. 143; [2004] 1 P. & C.R. DG12; *The Times*, November 20, 2003; *Independent*, November 25, 2003, HL; affirming [2001] EWCA Civ 212; [2001] Env L.R. 44; (2001) 3 L.G.L.R. 33; [2001] 9 E.G.C.S. 228; (2001) 98(9) L.S.G. 42; [2001] Env L.R. D11; *Daily Telegraph*, March 6, 2001 .... 38–02, 38–05, 38–12, 38–14.1, 39–02—39–05

Triodos Bank NV v Ashley Dobbs [2005] EWCA Civ 630; [2005] 2 C.L.C. 95; *The Times*, May 30, 2005, CA (Civ Div) 11–15

Turkey v Awadh [2005] EWCA Civ 382 17–03

Turner v News Group Newspapers Ltd [2005] EWHC 892; [2005] E.M.L.R. 25, QBD . 28–48

United Trading Corp SA v Allied Arab Bank, *sub nom.* Murray Clayton v Rafidair Bank [1985] 2 Lloyd's Rep. 554 (Note) 8–05

Various Ledward Claimants v Kent and Medway HA [2003] EWHC 2551; [2004] 1 Costs L.R. 101 37–02

Verjee v CICB Bank and Trust Co (Channel Islands) Ltd [2001] Lloyd's Rep. Bank. 279 .... 5–06.1

Viscount De L'Isle v Times Newspapers [1988] 1 W.L.R. 49; [1987] 3 All E.R. 499; (1988) 85(6) L.S.G. 38; (1988) 132 S.J. 54 28–30

W v Commissioner of Police of the Metropolis [2000] 1 W.L.R. 1607; [2000] 4 All E.R. 934; [2000] I.C.R. 1064; [2000] I.R.L.R. 720; [2001] P.I.Q.R. P6; (2000) 97(39) L.S.G. 42; (2000) 144 S.J.L.B. 248; *The Times*, August 1, 2000; *Independent*, November 6, 2000 (C.S.), HL; reversing [1997] I.C.R. 1073; [1997] I.R.L.R. 589; *The Times*, July 21, 1997, CA (Civ Div); affirming [1995] I.C.R. 510; [1995] I.R.L.R. 531 .... 2–06B

WISE Underwriting Agency Ltd v Grupo Nacional Provincial SA [2004] EWCA Civ 962; [2004] 2 All E.R. (Comm) 613; [2004] 2 Lloyd's Rep. 483; [2004] Lloyd's Rep. I.R. 764; (2004) 148 S.J.L.B. 913, CA (Civ Div); reversing [2003] EWHC 3038; [2004] 1 All E.R. (Comm) 495 .... 58–06.3

TABLE OF CASES

Wainwright v Home Office, *sub nom.* Wainwright v Secretary of State for the Home Department; Secretary of State for the Home Department v Wainwright [2003] UKHL 53; [2004] 2 A.C. 406; [2003] 3 W.L.R. 1137; [2003] 4 All E.R. 969; [2004] U.K.H.R.R. 154; 15 B.H.R.C. 387; (2003) 100(45) L.S.G. 30; (2003) 147 S.J.L.B. 1208; *The Times*, October 20, 2003, HL; affirming [2001] EWCA Civ 2081; [2002] Q.B. 1334; [2002] 3 W.L.R. 405; [2003] 3 All E.R. 943; (2002) 99(9) L.S.G. 31; (2002) 146 S.J.L.B. 18; *The Times*, January 4, 2002; *Independent*, January 23, 2002 38–11

—— v Secretary of State for the Home Department; Secretary of State for the Home Department v Wainwright. *See* Wainwright v Home Office

Watford Electronics Ltd v Sanderson CFL Ltd [2001] EWCA Civ 317; [2001] 1 All E.R. (Comm) 696; [2001] B.L.R. 143; (2001) 3 T.C.L.R. 14; [2002] F.S.R. 19; [2001] Masons C.L.R. 57; (2001) 98(18) L.S.G. 44; *The Times*, March 9, 2001, CA (Civ Div); reversing [2000] 2 All E.R. (Comm) 984 27–07

West Bromwich Building Society v Wilkinson. *See* Wilkinson v West Bromwich Building Society

Wilkinson v West Bromwich Building Society, *sub nom.* West Bromwich Building Society v Wilkinson [2005] UKHL 44; [2005] 1 W.L.R. 2303; [2005] 4 All E.R. 97; [2005] 27 E.G.C.S. 221; (2005) 102(28) L.S.G. 32; *The Times*, July 4, 2005; *Independent*, July 7, 2005, HL; affirming [2004] EWCA Civ 1063; [2004] C.P. Rep. 42; (2004) 101(36) L.S.G. 34; (2004) 148 S.J.L.B. 975; [2004] N.P.C. 134; [2004] 2 P. & C.R. DG22; *The Times*, October 5, 2004, CA (Civ Div) 13 05

Williams v Southampton Institute; Dawson v Stonham Housing Association; Kingston Upon Hull City Council v Dunnachie (No.1). *See* Dunnachie v Kingston upon Hull City Council

Wong v Igen Ltd (formerly Leeds Careers Guidance), *sub nom.* Emokpae v Chamberlin Solicitors; Webster v Brunel University; Igen Ltd (formerly Leeds Careers Guidance) v Wong; Brunel University v Webster; Chambelin Solicitors v Emokpae [2005] EWCA Civ 142; [2005] 3 All E.R. 812; [2005] I.C.R. 931; [2005] I.R.L.R. 258; (2005) 102(13) L.S.G. 28; (2005) 149 S.J.L.B. 264; *The Times*, March 3, 2005, CA (Civ Div) 35–04

Workington Harbour and Dock Board v Trade Indemnity Co Ltd. *See* Trade Indemnity Co Ltd v Workington Harbour and Dock Board (No.1)

X (Minors) v Bedfordshire CC, *sub nom.* M (A Minor) v Newham LBC; E (A Minor) v Dorset CC (Appeal); Christmas v Hampshire CC (Duty of Care); Keating v Bromley LBC (No.2) [1995] 2 A.C. 633; [1995] 3 W.L.R. 152; [1995] 3 All E.R. 353; [1995] 2 F.L.R. 276; [1995] 3 F.C.R. 337; 94 L.G.R. 313; (1995) 7 Admin. L.R. 705; [1995] Fam. Law 537; (1996) 160 L.G. Rev 123; (1996) 160 L.G. Rev 103; (1995) 145 N.L.J. 993; *The Times*, June 30, 1995; *Independent*, June 30, 1995, HL; affirming [1994] 2 W.L.R. 554; [1994] 4 All E.R. 602; [1994] 1 F.L.R. 431; 92 L.G.R. 427; [1994] Fam. Law 434; (1994) 144 N.L.J. 357; *The Times*, March 3, 1994; *Independent*, February 24, 1994; *Guardian*, February 28, 1994, CA (Civ Div); affirming [1993] 2 F.L.R. 575; [1994] P.I.Q.R. P515; [1993] Fam. Law 575; (1993) 143 N.L.J. 1783; *The Times*, November 24, 1993; *Independent*, December 23, 1993 .... 2–06B

Yorkshire Bank Plc v Tinsley [2004] EWCA Civ 816; [2004] 1 W.L.R. 2380; [2004] 3 All E.R. 463; [2004] 2 F.L.R. 1079; [2004] Fam. Law 719; [2004] 28 E.G.C.S. 176; (2004) 101(27) L.S.G. 32; (2004) 148 S.J.L.B. 822; [2004] 2 P. & C.R. DG19; *The Times*, August 12, 2004; *Independent*, July 1, 2004 .... 17–05A

Table of Statutes

1925
    Land Registration Act (15 &
        16 Geo. 5, c.21)
        s.82 .... 84–03, 84–U3
        s.138 .... 84–03, 84–U3

1954
    Landlord and Tenant Act (2 &
        3 Eliz. 2, c.56)
        s.23(1A) 78–U2
          (3) 78–07
        s.24 .... 78–U2, 78–U7, 88–U10
          (1) 78–02
        s.24A............. 78–03, 78–U4
        s.24C 78–03
          (2) 78–08
          (3) 78–08
        s.24D 78–03
        s.25 .... 78–U2, 78–U4, 78–U8, 88–U10
        s.26............. 78–U2, 88–U10
          (6) 78–U4
        s.28 .... 88–U10
        s.29(2) .... 78–02, 78–06—78–07
        s.29A(2) 78–U2
        s.29B(1) 78–U2
          (2) 78–U2
        s.30 78–02
          (1) 78–05
          (1A) 78–05
          (1B) 78–05
          (1C) 78–05
        s.31A 78–U2
        s.32(2) 78–U4
        s.37(3A) 78–05
          (3B) 78–05
          (4) 78–10
        s.38A............. 78–04, 78–U7
        s.41 .... 78–U2
        s.42 .... 78–U2

1967
    Misrepresentation Act (c.7)
        s.2(1) 4–06

1970
    Equal Pay Act (c.41) 35–01.2

1971
    Animals Act (c.22)
        s.2(2) 2–01

1972
    European Communities Act (c.68)
        s.2 35–04

1974
    Consumer Credit Act (c.39)........... 19–03, 19–25

1974
    Consumer Credit Act—*cont.*
        s.55 19–18

1976
    Race Relations Act (c.74) . 35–04
        s.1(1A) 35–04
        s.3A 35–04
          (1) 54–03
        s.65(2) 35–04

1977
    Unfair Contract Terms Act (c.50)........ 24–01.1, 24–37.2
        s.12 .... 24–01.1

1980
    Limitation Act (c.58)
        s.2 2–01
        s.11............... 2–01, 75–T14
        s.14 .... 72–04.1

1983
    Matrimonial Homes Act (c.19) 13–07.2

1984
    County Courts Act (c.28)
        s.69 .... 72–S6.1

1985
    Companies Act (c.6)
        s.46(2) 6–03
        s.162A 10–04
        s.349(9) 6–03
    Landlord and Tenant Act (c.70) 87–01
        s.20 90–02
        s.20ZA 90–02

1986
    Insolvency Act (c.45)
        s.213 49–07

1988
    Copyright, Designs and Patents Act (c.48) 67–02
    Road Traffic Act (c.52) ... 59–02

1992
    Trade Union and Labour Relations (Consolidation) Act (c.52) 34–08
        s.174 34–08
        s.175 34–08
        s.176 34–08
        s.230(2A) 33–10
          (2B) 33–10
        s.232B 33–10
        s.234A(3) 33–10
          (5A) 33–10
        s.244 33–08

1993
    Leasehold Reform, Housing and Urban Development Act (c.28)
        s.13 .... 87–U10

Table of Statutes

1994
Trade Marks Act (c.26)
  s.10(3) 68–01.1

1995
Disability Discrimination Act (c.50) 35–04, 54–03
  s.3B 54–03
  s.56(3) 35–04

1996
Employment Rights Act (c.18)
  s.98A 31–03.3
  s.123(1) 31–03.4
  s.203 .... 31–03.5
Family Law Act (c.27) ... 13–07.2

1997
Protection from Harassment Act (c.40) 54–02.2, 71–07
  s.1 .... 54–02.1, 71–S17A
  s.3 .... 54–02.2, 71–S17A
  s.7(3) 54–02.1

1998
Late Payment of Commercial Debts (Interest) Act (c.20) 12–02
Human Rights Act (c.42) . 78–U2
  s.6 57–04
  s.12(4) 29–02A

2000
Financial Services and Markets Act (c.8)
  s.28 10–13

2002
Land Registration Act (c.9)
  84–03
  s.65 84–03
  s.115 96–09
  Sch.4 84–03
Commonhold and Leasehold Reform Act (c.15) ... 87–01, 90–02
  s.173 .... 87–U7
  s.174 .... 87–U7
  s.175 .... 87–U7

2002 Commonhold and Leasehold Reform Act—*cont.*
  s.176 .... 87–U7
  Sch.12 .... 87–U7
Employment Act (c.22) ... 31–03.3
  s.30 .... 31–03.3
  s.31(3) 31–03.3
  s.32 .... 31–03.3
    (6) 31–03.3
  s.34 .... 31–03.3
  Sch.2 .... 31–03.3
Nationality, Immigration and Asylum Act (c.41) ... 57–05
  s.82(2) 57–05
  s.85(4) 57–04
  s.92 57–02
  s.94 .... 57–03.1
  s.103A 57–02, 57–03.1, 57–05
    (1) 57–02, 57–05
    (2) 57–02
    (3) 57–02
    (8) 57–02
    (9) 57–02
  s.103B 57–02
    (5) 57–02
  s.103C(1) 57–02
  s.103E 57–02

2004
Asylum and Immigration (Treatment of Claimants, etc.) Act (c.19) ... 57–01—57–02
  s.8(4) 57–04
  Sch.2 57–02
  Sch.3 .... 57–03.1
Employment Relations Act (c.24) 33–10, 34–08
  Pt I 34–08
  Pt II 34–08
  Pt III 34–08
  Pt V 34–08
  s.33 34–08
  s.48 34–08

Table of Statutory Instruments

1988
Loading and Unloading of Fishing Vessels Regulations (SI 1988/1656) . . . 71–07.1

1989
Health and Safety Information for Employees Regulations (SI 1989/682)
reg.4 . . . . 71–S17A

1992
Management of Health and Safety at Work Regulations (SI 1992/2051) 71–07, 71–S17A
reg.3 . . . . 71–S17A
reg.4 . . . . 71–S17A
reg.5 . . . . 71–S17A
reg.6 . . . . 71 S17A
reg.7 . . . . 71–S17A
reg.8 . . . . 71–S17A
reg.11 . . . . 71–S17A
reg.12 . . . . 71–S17A

1993
Commercial Agents (Council Directive) Regulations (SI 1993/3053) 20–01.2

1994
Employment Tribunals Extension of Jurisdiction (England and Wales) Order (SI 1994/1623)
art.4 31–02
Employment Tribunals Extension of Jurisdiction (Scotland) Order (SI 1994/1624)
art.4 31–02

1996
Health and Safety (Consultation with Employees) Regulations (SI 1996/1513)
reg.3 . . . . 71–S17A
Work in Compressed Air Regulations (SI 1996/1656) 71–07.1

1997
Fire Precautions (Workplace) Regulations (SI 1997/1840) 71–07.1

1998
Working Time Regulations (SI 1998/1833). 71–07, 71–S17A
reg.4 . . . . 71–S17A
reg.8 . . . . 71–S17A

1998 Working Time Regulations—cont.
reg.10 . . . . 71–S17A
reg.11 . . . . 71–S17A
reg.12 . . . . 71–S17A
reg.13 . . . . 71–S17A

1999
Quarries Regulations (SI 1999/2024) 71–07.1
Management of Health and Safety at Work Regulations (SI 1999/3242) . 71–07
reg.3 . . . . 71–S11A, 71–S17A
reg.4 . . . . 71–S17A
reg.5 . . . . 71–S17A
reg.6 . . . . 71–S17A
reg.8 . . . . 71–S17A
reg.10 . . . . 71–S17A
reg.13 . . . . 71–S17A
reg.14 . . . . 71–S17A
Sch.1 . . . . 71–S17A

2000
Consumer Protection (Distance Selling) Regulations (SI 2000/2334). . 18–08.1, 19–12.1, 19–D16— 19–D17, 19–D58.1, 24–09.2, 24–D59, 25–17, 25–D32
reg.10 . . . . 19–12.1, 19–D58.1, 24–09.2, 24–D59
reg.13 . . . . 19–12.1
reg.14 . . . . 19–12.1, 24–09.2
reg.15 . . . . 19–12.1, 19–D58.1, 24–09.2
reg.16 . . . . 19–12.1, 24–09.2
reg.17 . . . . 19–12.1, 24–09.2
reg.20 . . . . 19–D58.1, 24–D59
reg.21 . . . . 19–12.1, 19–D16—19–D17
reg.24 . . . . 25–17, 25–D32

2001
Civil Procedure (Amendment) Rules (SI 2001/256) 13–01.1
Employment Tribunals (Constitution and Rules of Procedure) Regulations (SI 2001/1171) . 31–01
Financial Services and Markets Act 2000 (Exemption) Order (SI 2001/1201) 10–09
Financial Services and Markets Act 2000 (Financial Promotion) Order (SI 2001/1335) 10–07

Table of Statutory Instruments

2002

Financial Services and Markets Act 2000 (Financial Promotion and Miscellaneous Amendments) Order (SI 2002/1310).	10–09
Financial Services and Markets Act 2000 (Regulated Activities) (Amendment) (No.2) Order (SI 2002/1776).	10–04
Financial Services and Markets Act 2000 (Fourth Motor Insurance Directive) Regulations (SI 2002/2706)	10–10
Dangerous Substances and Explosive Atmospheres Regulations (SI 2002/2776)	71–07.1

2003

Financial Services and Markets Act 2000 (Exemption) (Amendment) Order (SI 2003/47)	10–09
Rules of the Air (Amendment) Regulations (SI 2003/64) ...	3–05
Financial Services and Markets Act 2000 (Regulated Activities) (Amendment) (No.1) Order (SI 2003/1475).	10–04
Financial Services and Markets Act 2000 (Regulated Activities) (Amendment) (No.2) Order (SI 2003/1476).	10–04
Race Relations Act 1976 (Amendment) Regulations (SI 2003/1626) .	35–04
Employment Equality (Religion or Belief) Regulations (SI 2003/1660)	35–04, 54–03
reg.5	54–03
reg.33	35–04
Employment Equality (Sexual Orientation) Regulations (SI 2003/1661) ...	35–04, 54–03
reg.5	54–03
reg.33	35–04
Disability Discrimination Act 1995 (Amendment) Regulations (SI 2003/1673)	54–03
Financial Services and Markets Act 2000 (Exemption) (Amendment) (No.2) Order (SI 2003/1675).	10–09
Service Charges (Consultation Requirements) (England) Regulations (SI 2003/1987)	90–02
Leasehold Valuation Tribunals (Procedure) (England) Regulations (SI 2003/2099)	87–U7
Financial Services and Markets Act 2000 (Regulated Activities) (Amendment) (No.3) Order (SI 2003/2822).	10–04
Regulatory Reform (Business Tenancies) (England and Wales) Order (SI 2003/3096)	78–01

2004

Offshore Installations (Safety Zones) Order (SI 2004/343)	71–07.1
Carriage of Dangerous Goods and Use of Transportable Pressure Equipment Regulations (SI 2004/568)	71–07.1
Leasehold Valuation Tribunals (Procedure) (Wales) Regulations (SI 2004/681)	87–U7
Employment Act 2002 (Dispute Resolution) Regulations (SI 2004/752)	31–03.3
reg.3	31–03.3
reg.4	31–03.3
reg.5	31–03.3
reg.7	31–03.3
reg.11	31–03.3
reg.15	31–03.3
Consumer Credit (Disclosure of Information) Regulations (SI 2004/1481) ...	18–08.2, 19–18
Consumer Credit (Agreements) (Amendment) Regulations (SI 2004/1482) ...	18–08.2, 19–19, 19–D50—19–D51
Consumer Credit (Early Settlement) Regulations (SI 2004/1483) .	18–08.2, 19–D5
Consumer Credit (Advertisements) Regulations (SI 2004/1484)	18–08.2
Financial Services and Markets Act 2000 (Regulated Activities) (Amendment) Order (SI 2004/1610)	10–04

TABLE OF STATUTORY INSTRUMENTS

Offshore Installations (Safety Zones) (No.3) Order (SI 2004/1746) 71–07.1
Employment Tribunals (Constitution and Rules of Procedure) Regulations (SI 2004/1861) . 31–01—31–03, 35–01.1, 35–03
  reg.3 .... 31–03.2
  Sch.1 .... 31–01, 31–03
    r.1 31–01
    r.3 31–03
    r.4 .... 31–01—31–03.1
    r.6 31–03
    r.7 .... 31–01—31–02
    r.8 31–03
    r.33 .... 31–03.1
Financial Services (Distance Marketing) Regulations (SI 2004/2095) 18–08.1, 19–12.1
Financial Services and Markets Act 2000 (Regulated Activities) (Amendment) (No.2) Order (SI 2004/2737). 10–04
Consumer Credit (Enforcement, Default and Termination Notices) (Amendment) Regulations (SI 2004/3237) 18–08.2
Financial Services and Markets Act 2000 (Designated Professional Bodies) (Amendment) Order (SI 2004/3352). 10–09
Life Assurance Consolidation Directive (Consequential Amendments) Regulations (SI 2004/3379) . 10–04
Control of Substances Hazardous to Health (Amendment) Regulations (SI 2004/3386) . 71–07.1

2005

Asylum and Immigration Tribunal (Procedure) Rules (SI 2005/230) 57–03.1
  r.7 57–02
  r.31 57–05
Financial Services and Markets Act 2000 (Exemption) (Amendment) Order (SI 2005/592) 10–09

Financial Services and Markets Act 2000 (Regulated Activities) (Amendment) Order (SI 2005/593) 10–04
Work at Height Regulations (SI 2005/735) 71–07.1
  reg.4 .... 71–S11A
  reg.5 .... 71–S11A
  reg.6 .... 71–S11A
  reg.7 .... 71–S11A
  reg.8 .... 71–S11A
  reg.9 .... 71–S11A
  reg.10 .... 71–S11A
  reg.11 .... 71–S11A
  reg.12 .... 71–S11A
  reg.13 .... 71–S11A
  reg.14 .... 71–S35A
  Sch. 71–S11A
  Sch.1 .... 71–S11A
  Sch.2 .... 71–S11A
  Sch.3 Pt 1 .... 71–S11A
    Pt 2 .... 71–S11A
  Sch.4 .... 71–S11A
  Sch.5 Pt 1 .... 71–S11A
    Pt 2 .... 71–S11A
    Pt 3 .... 71–S11A
    Pt 4 .... 71–S11A
    Pt 5 .... 71–S11A
  Sch.6 .... 71–S11A
Equipment and Protective Systems Intended for Use in Potentially Explosive Atmospheres (Amendment) Regulations (SI 2005/830) .. 71–07.1
Manufacture and Storage of Explosives Regulations (SI 2005/1082) 71–07.1
Control of Vibration at Work Regulations (SI 2005/1093).... 71–07.1, 71–S21
  reg.4 .... 71–S21
  reg.5 .... 71–S21
  reg.6 .... 71–S21
  reg.7 .... 71–S21
  reg.8 .... 71–S21
Rules of the Air (Amendment) Regulations (SI 2005/1110) . 3–05
Financial Services and Markets Act 2000 (Regulated Activities) (Amendment) (No.2) Order (SI 2005/1518). 10–04
Financial Services and Markets Act 2000 (Financial Promotion) Order (SI 2005/1529) 10–07

xxxiii

Part A

ASSAULT, FALSE IMPRISONMENT AND MALICIOUS PROSECUTION

SECTION 2: ASSAULT, FALSE IMPRISONMENT AND MALICIOUS PROSECUTION

(1) Assault

Cause of action.

Add at end of second paragraph:

In *Marper v Chief Constable of South Yorkshire*, unreported, 2004, the House of Lords **2–01** considered the lawfulness of an intimate sample retention policy for unconvicted persons. Their Lordships held that the Chief Constable's retention policy did not breach Art.8 of the European Convention on Human Rights.

In the last paragraph, after citation for Pollard v Chief Constable of West Yorkshire Police, add:

See further Ch.20, Section 2, para.9 of the Association of Chief Police Officers (ACPO) Police Dog Training and Care Manual which requires police dog handlers to submit a report on the use of force where a prisoner is injured by a dog. If such a report is made (as it should be) where there is an attack by a dog, then ordinarily it ought to be disclosed in accordance with CPR Pt 31. Chapter 20, Section 5, para.17, of the Police Dog Training and Care Manual imposes a duty on a Chief Officer of Police that "when the handler deploys with the dog they are duty-bound to maintain control of the dog at all times." Where claimants allege that they have been attacked by a police dog, practitioners should also consider whether s.2(2) of the Animals Act 1971 might apply. Thus, if a claimant is bitten by a police dog which is unusually fierce and this characteristic is known to the police dog handler or the defendant at the time of the assault, then the police would potentially be liable under s.2(2)(b) of the 1971 Act.

Add at end:

In *Lister v Hesley Hall Ltd* [2002] 1 A.C. 215 the House of Lords considered the issue of vicarious liability and whether damages ought to be awarded where there was a sufficient connection between the work that the primary tort feasor had been employed to do and the acts of abuse he had committed, and whether those acts fell within the scope of his employment and, accordingly, whether the defendants should be held vicariously liable for them. Having set out the test, Lord Steyn at para.29 left open the argument about whether an employee was under a duty to report his (own) wrong-doing to his employers and whether liability might be found where there was a failure to report. See *C v Middlesbrough BC* [2004] EWCA Civ 1746 where the Court of Appeal considered the appellant's claim for vicarious liability against a local authority and whether that was a claim for trespass to the person falling within the non-extendable time limit prescribed in s.2 of the Limitation Act 1980 or whether s.11 of the Act applied. It appears that the courts are trying to narrow the potential for extending the scope of the duty. See the reference to the House of Lords decision in *Brooks* below.

(2) False Imprisonment

Cause of action.

In the first paragraph, after "(Bird v Jones (1845) 7 Q.B. 742).", add:

In *Laporte v Chief Constable of Gloucestershire Constabulary* [2004] EWCA Civ 1639 **2–03** the Court of Appeal considered the defendant's powers to prevent protestors attending a demonstration at RAF Fairford and force them to return to London. The claimants advanced arguments, *inter alia*, that the defendant had breached their rights under Arts 5, 10 and 11 of the European Convention on Human Rights. The court considered the extent to which the police had power to undertake preventative action short of arrest, including temporary detention, for what was described as "transitory" detention. The court found that detention for 2½ hours, that being the return journey to London, could not be described as transitory detention and was accordingly unlawful. Nonetheless, the Court of Appeal refused to engage Art.5.

Add at end of first paragraph:

In *Cummings v Chief Constable of Northumbria Police* [2003] EWCA Civ 1844 the court considered whether there were reasonable grounds for officers to arrest and/or whether they acted in accordance with *Wednesbury* principles after they arrested the claimant in circumstances where only one of them could have committed the offence. Interestingly, in this case the claimants all worked with the police, were known to them and were of previous good character. The court considered arguments and accepted that when exercising powers of arrest the police had to have in mind Art.5, guaranteeing the right to liberty. With some reservation the Court of Appeal found that the arrest of the claimants was lawful. Their Lordships expressed an opinion that there would be cases where it might be necessary to detain a large group of suspects even though they would not all have committed an offence. See further the decision of the Court of Appeal in *Mohamed Al Fayed v Commissioner of Police of the Metropolis* [2004] EWCA Civ 1579.

In the third paragraph, after "Clubb v Wimpey & Co. [1936] 1 All E.R. 69).", add:

In *Taylor v Chief Constable of Thames Valley Police* [2004] EWCA Civ 858 the Court of Appeal reconsidered whether the claimant had been sufficiently informed of the reasons for his arrest. The court held that the relevant principles were helpfully restated in *Fox, Campbell and Hartley v United Kingdom* (1991) 13 E.H.R.R. 157 at para.40. Sedley L.J. held that attention had to be given to whether the words "under arrest" might be sufficient for an adult but would not be for a child. In this case, their Lordships found that the officer telling a 10-year-old boy that he was being arrested "on suspicion of violent disorder" will not always be an adequate description of the material offence. The court held that the legal names of some of the crimes are not self-explanatory. This case is also important as the Court of Appeal additionally dealt with the issue of length of detention. The court approved the *dicta* of Donaldson M.R. in *Mercer v Chief Constable of Lancashire Police* [1991] 1 W.L.R. 367 and reiterated the finding that it is for the police to justify the whole period of detention "minute-by-minute and hour-by-hour". The court held that even a short delay which cannot be accounted for may be found to be unreasonable.

(3) Malicious Prosecution

Add at end of first paragraph:

2–05.2 The decision in *Paul v Chief Constable of Humberside Police* [2004] EWCA Civ 308 is an important decision for those acting for claimants, as the Court of Appeal indicated that evidence of malice or bad faith did not necessarily have to flow from primary evidence as in many cases such evidence is hard, if not impossible, to obtain or elicit in cross-examination.

(4A) Misfeasance in Public Office

Add at end:

2–06A In *Keegan v Chief Constable of Merseyside Police* [2003] 1 W.L.R. 2187 the claimant's case was that the defendant's officers had maliciously procured a search warrant, or were reckless as to the exercise of their powers, where they had obtained a search warrant without ascertaining that the alleged suspects had vacated the property a number of months earlier. The court wrestled with the two competing interests: that an Englishman's home is said to be his castle and the policy consideration of not hampering the police in the proper investigation of criminal offences. In refusing the appeal, the Court of Appeal restated that the test for misfeasance was a high one and the burden of establishing it never shifted from the claimant.

SUPPLEMENT 1 — NOVEMBER, 2005

Add after para.2–06A:

(4B) Negligence

In *Brooks v Commissioner of Police for the Metropolis* [2005] 1 W.L.R. 1495 the House **2–06B**
of Lords considered whether Duwayne Brooks, who was a friend of and present at the racist killing of Stephen Lawrence, ought to be permitted to bring a claim in negligence against the Commissioner. The House of Lords considered whether there was sufficient proximity between the Commissioner and those for whom he was vicariously responsible on the one hand and Mr Brooks on the other and whether it would give rise to the following duties:

(i) to take reasonable steps to assess whether Mr Brooks was a victim of crime and then to accord him appropriate protection, support, assistance and treatment;
(ii) to take sufficient steps to afford Mr Brooks the protection, assistance and support afforded to eye witnesses of serious crime;
(iii) to attach reasonable weight to the witness evidence given by Mr Brooks and to act on that accordingly and, in all the circumstances, whether it would be fair, just and reasonable to hold the Commissioner liable.

In this important decision the House of Lords reviewed *Hill v Chief Constable of West Yorkshire Police* [1989] A.C. 53; *X (Minors) v Bedfordshire CC* [1995] 2 A.C. 633; *Barrett v Enfield LBC* [1999] 3 W.L.R. 79; *W v Commissioner of Police of the Metropolis* [2000] 1 W.L.R. 1607; *Dorset Co. Ltd v Home Office* [1970] A.C. 104 and other leading cases. Whilst the House of Lords held that the law regarding the liability of the police in tort was not set in stone, their Lordships reiterated that the three duties of care advanced were conclusively ruled out by the principle in *Hill*. The Commissioner's appeal was allowed. Lord Rodger of Earlsferry held in an *obiter* comment that the decisions in *Elguzouli-Daf v Commissioner of Police of the Metropolis* [1995] Q.B. 335 and *Kumar v Commissioner of Police of the Metropolis*, unreported, January 31, 1995, held that the Crown Prosecution Service and the police owed no separate duty of care to a defendant against whom they instituted and maintained proceedings. Whilst Lord Steyne refused to rule out that there might be circumstances of "outrageous negligence" by the police which would fall beyond the reach of the *Hill* principle, those would be exceptional cases and would have to be considered by the courts on a case-by-case basis if and when they occur.

(5) Pleadings

Add at end of second paragraph:

In a number of recent cases the Court of Appeal has considered the extent to which it **2–07**
can compel parties to engage in mediation or alternative dispute resolution. Practitioners affected by this should look at the provisions of CPR r.1.4.11 and the helpful notes in Vol.1 of *Civil Procedure Rules*, 2005. Those practising in London may already be familiar with the Practice Direction issued by the Presiding Judge at Central London County Court requiring parties in police cases to engage in mediation.

In the second paragraph, after the citation for Thompson v Commission of Police for the Metropolis, add:

There have been very few quantum decisions of note since the 15th edition main text **2–07.1**
was produced. Practitioners should bear in mind that the quantum brackets are now fairly old and require updating. There is an inflation table index in *Facts and Figures* which is useful. As to quantum cases generally, Legal Action reports first instance decisions on a regular basis, though these of course are not binding, though they are useful as a quantum benchmark.

Part B

AVIATION

Section 3: Aviation

Overflight.

Add at end:

In *Dennis v Ministry of Defence* [2003] EWHC 793, QB it was held that the noise of Harrier aircraft operating from RAF Wittering amounted to a nuisance and a breach of Art.8 of the European Convention on Human Rights. The public interest in RAF training meant that an injunction was inappropriate but the court awarded damages of £950,000 to the landowner who brought the action. **3–02**

Mid-air Collision.

Add at end:

Now see Rules of Air (Amendment) Regulations 2003 (SI 2003/64) and Rules of Air (Amendment) Regulations 2005 (SI 2005/1110). **3–05**

Defences

Defence to claim for psychiatric damage caused by witnessing an air crash

Add at end of note 1:
No such appeal has been reported. **3–B10**

Section 4: Carriage by Air

(1) Particulars of Claim

General.

Add at end:

The Montreal Convention 1999 came into force in some countries on November 4, 2003. It came into force in the United Kingdom and in other EU Member States on June 28, 2004. The Montreal Convention 1999 was implemented in EU Member States by European Council Regulation EC 889/2002. In considering any claim concerning international carriage by air it is necessary to identify the applicable international convention.   **4–01**

The Warsaw Convention Regime.

Add at end:

Except as stated in para.4–16, below, the commentary in respect of the Amended Convention is broadly applicable to the Montreal Convention 1999.   **4–03**

(2) Rights of Action and Pleading

Liability of the Carrier.

Add at end of fourth paragraph, after the citation for Re: Deep Vein Thrombosis and Air Travel Group Litigation:

Re: Deep Vein Thrombosis and Air Travel Group Litigation is also reported at [2003] 3 W.L.R. 956, and is on appeal to the House of Lords. The Supreme Court of the United States has, by a majority decision, rejected the argument that only an affirmative act can be an event constituting an "accident" as used in Art.17 of the Amended Convention (*Olympic Airways v Husain* 124 SCt 1221 (2004)). In the *Husain* case, a passenger died from an allergic reaction to cigarette smoke, having been seated close to the smoking section of an aircraft. The Supreme Court held that the refusal on three occasions by a cabin attendant to seat elsewhere the passenger was an event constituting an accident under Art.17.   **4–06**

Add at end:

In any claim for delay it will be necessary to refer to the provisions of the European Council Regulation 261/2004 ("the Regulation") which came into force on February 17, 2005 in all EU Member States. The Regulation is directly applicable in each Member State. Depending on particular circumstances, the Regulation requires a carrier to provide passengers who are refused carriage on a flight (usually denied boarding because they have been "bumped off" through overbooking) or who have been delayed significantly (more than two hours for flights of up to 1,500km; or more than three hours for flights between 1,500 and 3,500kms; or more than four hours for other flights), or whose flights are cancelled, a combination of compensation, assistance, refunds and re-routing to the final destination. The Regulation is applicable to scheduled and non-scheduled flights. Carriers are obliged to explain to passengers the rights that they have pursuant to the Regulation. Any payment made under the provisions of the Regulation are made without prejudice to a passenger's rights for further compensation, although any payment made to a passenger pursuant to the Regulation can be deducted from any further compensation. It is a defence for a carrier to show that the denial of boarding, delay or cancellation was caused by extraordinary circumstances which could not have been avoided, such as weather conditions, security risks or strikes. A passenger who voluntarily surrenders the right to board a particular flight is not entitled to compensation under the Regulation. So far as the Warsaw Convention regime is concerned, the Regulation will apply to an Art.19 claim if the delay or cancellation occurs during the course of international carriage by air, that is, once the carrier has checked in a passenger. Where however, a carrier refuses carriage prior to check in then the Warsaw Convention regime will not apply. In this case the passenger will have rights under national law and the Regulation against the carrier. Such claims could include breach of contract and misrepresentation under s.2(1) of the Misrepresentation Act 1967.

The Regulation is subject to a judicial challenge which has been referred to the European Court of Justice. In the meantime however, it remains in force and applicable.

Claims against Tour Operators

Montreal Convention

Add after second sentence in third paragraph:

4–16 The carrier must deliver to the passenger a baggage identification tag for each piece of checked luggage, but it is no longer necessary for the carrier to make a note of the weight of the baggage, as this is irrelevant to the limit of compensation payable. The carrier is liable for the period when the checked baggage is on board the aircraft or when it is in the charge of the carrier (Art.17(2) of the Montreal Convention).

Add at end:

4–17 Jurisdiction: The Montreal Convention 1999 retains the four forums available under the Warsaw Convention in its different forms (Art.28 of the Amended Convention, for example) (that is court of domicile of the carrier, or of its principal place of business, or where it had a place of business through which the contract was made, or at the place of destination), and allows a new fifth forum in respect of passenger claims for death and injury. In such an instance claims can be brought in the territory of a state party to the Montreal Convention in which at the time of the accident the passenger has his or her principal and permanent residence and to or from which the carrier operates services for the carriage of passengers by air, either on its own aircraft or that of another operator by commercial agreement, and in which that carrier conducts business of carriage of passengers by air either from its own premises or from that of another carrier with which it has a commercial agreement (Art.33(2) of Montreal Convention 1999).

(3) Defences

Add after first sentence:

4–19 The Montreal Convention 1999 is now in force in the United Kingdom and in EU Member States (see para.4–01, above).

Add at end of third paragraph:

The Montreal Convention also confers on the carrier a defence that the damage to the baggage was caused by an inherent defect, or quality or vice of the baggage.

Part C

BANKING AND FINANCIAL SERVICES

SECTION 5: BANKERS

Replace note 3 with:
(3rd ed., 2004).   5–01

In the first paragraph, after "The Law Relating to Domestic Banking", add:

Warne and Elliott, *Banking Litigation*[1]
Note 1: (Sweet and Maxwell, 1999).

In the second paragraph, after note 10, add:

A bank notified of a freezing order owes a duty in tort to the party that has obtained the order to take care to prevent the dissipation of money in the frozen bank account.[1]
Note 1: *Customs & Excise Commissioners v Barclays Bank Plc* [2005] 1 W.L.R. 2082.

The operation of a bank account

Overdrawn accounts.

Replace note 19 with:
Chitty on Contract (29th ed., 2004), para.21–053.   5–03

Add at end of note 23:
; applied in *Emerald Meats (London) Ltd v AIB Group (UK) Plc* [2002] EWCA Civ 460.

Delete brackets around last sentence and add new footnote at end:
Note 1: An "unauthorised" borrowing rate would not normally be regarded as a penalty: see *Chitty on Contract* (29th ed., 2004), para.38–258. The position may be different in respect of a "default" rate of interest, applied by reason of customer's failure to repay an overdraft facility on demand; however, it has been held that there would be no justification in striking down as a penalty a modest increase in the applicable interest rate provided the higher rate took effect only from the date of default (*i.e.* if the rate is not applied retrospectively): *Lordsvale Finance Plc v Bank of Zambia* [1996] Q.B. 752.

Unauthorised payments

Breach of mandate.

Add at end of note 36:
(approved by the Court of Appeal in *Credit Agricole Indosuez v Muslim Commercial*   5–05
Bank Ltd [2000] 1 Lloyd's Rep. 275).

Replace note 37 with:
See generally, Brindle & Cox, *Law of Banking Payments* (2nd ed., Sweet & Maxwell, 2004), paras 3–070, 3–080.

Payments where the bank is on notice of fraud.

Add at end of note 40:
See also *Royal Products Ltd v Midland Bank Ltd* [1981] 2 Lloyd's Rep. 194 at 198.   5–06

Add at end of note 44:

5–06.1 ; *cf. Verjee v CICB Bank and Trust Co. (Channel Islands) Ltd* [2001] Lloyd's Rep. Bank. 279: the bank is unlikely to be put on notice of the possibility of fraud where the signatory to the account is the account-holder himself.

Mistaken payments

Replace the last sentence of the first paragraph and note 85 as follows:

5–11.1 A defendant who has changed his position in anticipation of the future receipt of a payment can equally rely on the defence of change of position.[1]

Note 1: *Dextra Bank and Trust Co. Ltd v Bank of Jamaica* [2002] 1 All E.R. (Comm) 193, PC; followed by the Court of Appeal in *Commerzbank v Gareth Price-Jones* [2003] EWCA Civ 1663.

The bank as a constructive trustee

Add at end of note 95:

5–12.1 See also *Polly Peck International Plc v Nadir (No.2)* [1992] 4 All E.R. 769, where, in relation to certain currency exchanges, it was found that the bank was exchanging currency in its own right and not as banker to its customer, and as such was held to be the recipient of the trust funds.

Add at end of note 98:

; followed by the Court of Appeal in *Criterion Properties Plc v Stratford UK Properties LLC* [2003] B.C.C. 50, where it was held that in applying the test, the court should have regard to the context and surrounding circumstances, including whether legal advice was taken, and whether it is dealing with a commercial transaction where decisions have to be taken quickly. See also *Niru Battery Manufacturing Co. v Milestone Trading Ltd* [2004] 1 All E.R. (Comm) 193, paras 156 and 188.

Section 6: Bills of Exchange

Parties and liabilities.

Add at end:

Section 349(9) of the Companies Act was discussed in *Fiorentino Comm Giuseppe Srl v Farnesi* [2005] EWHC 160; [2005] 2 All E.R. 737, ChD, where it was decided that to hold a person liable under the section it was not necessary that a cheque should have been presented for payment as there were circumstances dispensing with the need for presentation under s.46(2)(c) in that there was no reason to believe the cheque would be paid. **6–03**

SECTION 8: BONDS

Restraining payment on a performance bond.
Amend title as above, and replace paragraph and footnotes with:

In certain limited circumstances, the applicant for a performance bond may apply for an injunction restraining the beneficiary from making a claim upon or (if such a claim has already been made) restraining the obligor (*i.e.* the paying bank) from making payment under the bond.[1] The applicant faces a number of difficulties, however. The first is that he must establish a clear case of fraud to the knowledge of the party he is seeking to injunct: this will involve establishing that (i) the beneficiary has no right to payment under the bond; (ii) the beneficiary has no genuine belief in such right[2]; and (iii) (in the case of an injunction against the bank) the bank must have notice of the fraud. Where the application is being made against a bank the applicant faces a further difficulty, since in such a case damages will almost always be an adequate remedy for any breach of duty by the bank.[3]

8–05

The only other situation in which a beneficiary can be restrained from making a claim (or the bank restrained from making payment) under a performance bond is where there has not been strict compliance with the terms of the instrument. For example, the bond may stipulate that any demand upon it must be made within a specified period of time, or must be preceded by a letter requiring the applicant to remedy a breach of an underlying sale contract. If such formalities have not been adhered to, then payment will not be due under the bond according to its own terms, and hence a threatened claim or payment could be restrained by the court.

Note 1: Injunctions of this nature were upheld in *Themehelp Ltd v West* [1996] Q.B. 84 and *Kvaerner John Brown Ltd v Midland Bank Plc* [1998] C.L.C. 446; but see the criticisms of these decisions in *Czarnikow-Rionda v Standard Bank* [1999] 2 Lloyd's Rep. 187 at 190. For the Court of Appeal's general guidance as to the granting of without notice injunctions in this context see *Bolivinter Oil SA v Chase Manhattan Bank* [1984] 1Lloyd's Rep. 251.

Note 2: Lack of honest belief is fraud: *State Trading Corp of India Ltd v ED & F Man(Sugar) Ltd* [1981] Com. L.R. 235.

Note 3: *Harbottle (Mercantile) Ltd v National Westminster Bank* [1978] Q.B. 146 at 155, cited with approval in *United Trading Corp SA v Allied Arab Bank Ltd* [1985] 2 Lloyd's Rep. 554 (Note) at 565.

SECTION 9: CHEQUES

Add at end:

In *Thomas Cook New Zealand Limited v Commissioners of Inland Revenue* [2004] **9–01.2**
UKPC 53 the Privy Council, on appeal from the Court of Appeal of New Zealand ([2003]
2 N.Z.L.R. 296), had to consider the effect of the New Zealand Unclaimed Money Act
1971. While deciding the case on wholly different grounds, they doubted the correctness
of the Court of Appeal's conclusion that presentment was dispensed with in respect of a
stale cheque so as to give rise to a cause of action against the drawer from the point at
which it became stale, but did not analyse the issue (compare Byles on *Bills of Exchange
and Cheques* (27th ed.) at paras 29–08 and 29–09).

Section 10: Financial Services

Regulated Activity

Add at end:

The regulated activities specified for the purposes of s.22(1) have been amended by: **10–04**
(1) The Financial Services and Markets Act 2000 (Regulated Activities) (Amendment) (No.2) Order 2002 (SI 2002/1776), which excludes from regulated activities "information society services" (*i.e.* internet commerce) conducted from a state outside the EEA—in force August 21, 2002.
(2) The Financial Services and Markets Act 2000 (Regulated Activities) (Amendment) (No.1) Order 2003 (SI 2003/1475), covering regulated mortgage contracts and the activity of introducing the parties to such contracts—in force October 31, 2004.
(3) The Financial Services and Markets Act 2000 (Regulated Activities) (Amendment) (No.2) Order 2003 (SI 2003/1476), covering the activities of "insurance mediation", that is:
   (a) dealing in rights under a contract of insurance as agent;
   (b) arranging deals in rights under a contract of insurance;
   (c) assisting in the administration and performance of a contract of insurance;
   (d) advising on buying or selling rights under a contract of insurance;
   (e) agreeing to do any of the activities specified in sub-paras (a) to (d).
These provisions come into force on October 31, 2004 in respect of long-term care insurance and on January 14, 2005 for all other purposes.
(4) The Financial Services and Markets Act 2000 (Regulated Activities) (Amendment) (No.3) Order 2003 (SI 2003/2822) came into force on December 1, 2003. It provides that a company does not carry on a regulated activity by purchasing its own shares if the shares qualify as "treasury shares" within s.162A of the Companies Act 1985 (shares in a company purchased by the company itself with distributable profits).
(5) The Financial Services and Markets Act 2000 (Regulated Activities) (Amendment) Order 2004 (SI 2004/1610) disapplies s.49(2) of FSMA in relation to insurance mediation and regulated mortgage contract business. This amendment came into force on July 15, 2004.
(6) The Financial Services and Markets Act 2000 (Regulated Activities) (Amendment) (No.2) Order 2004 (SI 2004/2737) specifies the giving of basic advice on "stakeholder" pension schemes as a specified advice, and enables the provision of such advice by persons already having permission to give other forms of advice. In force April 6, 2005.

These provisions come into force on October 1, 2005:
(7) The Life Assurance Consolidation Directive (Consequential Amendments) Regulations 2004 (SI 2004/3379).
(8) The Financial Services and Markets Act 2000 (Regulated Activities) (Amendment) Order 2005 (SI 2005/593).
(9) The Financial Services and Markets Act 2000 (Regulated Activities) (Amendment) (No.2) Order 2005 (SI 2005/1518), which deregulates investment in unlisted companies by so-called "Business Angel-led Enterprise Capital Funds", which are collective investments schemes membership of which is limited to high-value companies, high value trusts and unincorporated associations and individuals, who are either "certified sophisticated investors" or "self-certified sophisticated investors".

Investment activity

Add at end of note 59:

10–07 The Financial Services and Markets Act 2000 (Financial Promotion) Order 2001 (SI 2001/1335) was revoked and replaced by the Financial Services and Markets Act 2000 (Financial Promotion) Order 2005 (SI 2005/1529) as from July 1, 2005.

Authorised and exempt persons

Add at end of note 64:

10–09 The Financial Services and Markets Act 2000 (Exemption) Order 2001 (SI 2001/1201) is further amended by (1) the Financial Services and Markets Act 2000 (Financial Promotion and Miscellaneous Amendments) Order 2002 (SI 2002/1310)—revoked with effect from July 1, 2005; (2) the Financial Services and Markets Act 2000 (Exemption) (Amendment) Order 2003 (SI 2003/47) adds the Bank for International Settlements as an exempted person from March 1, 2003; (3) the Financial Services and Markets Act 2000 (Exemption) (Amendment) (No.2) Order 2003 (SI 2003/1675) adds certain functions of local authorities to their exempt status and exempts registered social landlords and certain statutory housing bodies in respect of their activities in relation to mortgage contracts; (4) the Financial Services and Markets Act 2000 (Exemption) (Amendment) Order 2005 (SI 2005/592) adds the board of the Pension Protection Fund as an exempt person.

Add at end of note 68:

The Financial Services and Markets Act 2000 (Designated Professional Bodies) (Amendment) Order 2004 (SI 2004/3352) adds the Council for Licensed Conveyancers from January 14, 2005.

Proceedings covered in this title

Add at end:

10–10 A claimant need not be a private person if the rule alleged to have been contravened by a relevant authorised person (meaning a person authorised in relation to land-based motor insurance) requires compensation to be paid within a certain time or interest to be paid in any circumstances: Financial Services and Markets Act 2000 (Fourth Motor Insurance Directive) Regulations 2002 (SI 2002/2706).

Add at end:

10–13 This paragraph summarises the effect of FSMA s.28.

Section 11: Guarantees

Statute of Frauds.

Add at end of note 1:

Actionstrength was unsuccessfully appealed to the House of Lords: see [2003] UKHL 17; [2003] 2 A.C. 541. The speeches of Lords Bingham and Hoffmann provide useful summaries of the application of s.4.   **11–05**

Misrepresentation.

Add after first sentence:

See *National Westminster Bank Plc v Philip Bowles* [2005] EWHC 182, QB where a judgment in default of a defence entered against a guarantor by a bank was set aside. The basis for this was that the guarantor had an arguable case that the bank might not be entitled to enforce the guarantee either (1) because of the terms of an express agreement, or (2) on the principle that a surety was discharged if the creditor acted in bad faith towards him or was guilty of concealment amounting to misrepresentation or caused or connived at the default by the principal debtor in respect of which the guarantee was given.   **11–12**

Replace note 10 with:

See *County NatWest Ltd v Barton* [2002] 4 All E.R. 494 (Note), CA.

Discharge of guarantor by release of the principal debtor or by variation of the principal contract.

Add after second sentence:

For a modern example, see *Lloyds TSB Bank Plc v Norman Hayward* [2005] EWCA Civ 466, applying the rule in *Holme v Brunskill* (1877) 3 Q.B.D. 494.   **11–15**

Add at end:

However, it has been held that sums due from a company under a loan agreement are not covered by a guarantee of the sums due "under or pursuant to" an earlier loan agreement where the subsequent loan agreement is on substantially different terms and can not be regarded as an amendment or variation within the general purview of the original agreement: see *Triodos Bank NV v Ashley Dobbs* [2005] EWCA Civ 630, applying *Trade Indemnity Co. Ltd v Workington Harbour and Dock Board* [1937] A.C. 1.

Section 12: Money Lent

Replace note 21 with:
Chitty on Contracts (29th ed., 2004), para.38–223. **12–01**

Replace note 27 with:
Chitty, op. cit., para.38–238. **12–01.1**

Replace note 29 with:
Chitty, op. cit., para.38–238.

Replace note 31 with:
Chitty, op. cit., para.38–241.

Interest.

Replace note 34 with:
Chitty, op. cit., para.38–259. Note that the Late Payment of Commercial Debts (Interest) Act 1998 does not apply to lending contracts, but only to certain contracts for the supply of goods and services. **12–02**

At the end of note 35, for "para.38–251", substitute:
para.38–254

Novation.

Replace note 37 with:
Chitty, op. cit., para.19–085. **12–03**

Replace note 38 with:
Chitty, op.cit., para.3–173.

Defence alleging repayment of the loan

In note 43, for "(5th ed., 1998), pp.444–449", substitute:
(6th ed., 2002), paras 15–009 *et seq.* **12–C6**

SECTION 13: MORTGAGES AND CHARGES

Replace paragraph with:

13–01.1 The Civil Procedure (Amendment) Rules 2001 (SI 2001/256) introduced CPR Pt 55 which deals exclusively with possession claims. It came into force on October 15, 2001 and provides a new procedural code for possession claims. It applies to all possession claims issued on or after that date. Part 55 is accompanied by a Practice Direction and new forms have been drafted. Part 55 is essential reading before any pleading in relation to a mortgage claim is embarked upon.

Part 55 does not apply to claims issued before October 15, 2001—the rules in force immediately before that date apply as if they had not been amended or revoked.

Part 55 must be used where court proceedings include a possession claim brought by a landlord, a lender or a licensor. Part 55 must also be used in a claim brought against trespassers. A claim, which is not a possession claim, may be brought under the Pt 55 procedure if it is started in the same claim form as a possession claim.

Mortgage action

In the third paragraph, delete the words in brackets. **13–02**

Pleadings points for a mortgage claim

General.

Add after first sentence of third paragraph:

13–05 Recent cases include *Scottish Equitable Plc v Thompson* [2003] EWCA Civ 225; (2003) 7 E.G.C.S. 137 and *Wilkinson v West Bromwich Building Society* [2004] EWCA Civ 1063 (see also unsuccessful appeal to House of Lords at [2005] UKHL 44).

Add at end:

Failure to file or serve a defence does not prevent the defendant from taking part in the proceedings, although it may be taken into account when deciding what costs order to make: see CPR r.55.7.6.

Replace paras 13–06 to 13–07.2 with:

Where to bring the claim for possession.

13–06 The basic rule is that possession claims must be started in the county court for the district where the property is situated. However, a claim may be started in the High Court if there are exceptional circumstances (see PD55, paras 1.1–1.4). The value of the property and the amount of the financial claim may be relevant circumstances, but they alone will not normally justify starting the claim in the High Court. High Court claims for the possession of land subject to a mortgage will be assigned to the Chancery Division: see the Chancery Guide for further information, in particular Ch.21.

The claim form.

13–07 The claim form must be in prescribed form (PD55, para.2.6) and must be verified by a statement of truth. If proceedings are issued in the High Court, the claim form must be accompanied by a certificate stating the reasons for bringing the claim in the High Court, verified by a statement of truth.

Particulars of claim.

13–07.1 Particulars of claim must be filed and served with the claim form. All particulars of claim must:

(1) comply with CPR Pt 16. This means that they must contain a concise statement of facts and, if interest is sought, give details;

(2) identify the land to which the claim relates;
(3) state whether it is residential property;
(4) state the ground on which possession is claimed;
(5) give full details of any mortgage or tenancy agreement;
(6) give details of every person who, to the best of the claimant's knowledge, is in possession of the property; and
(7) include a copy of any written agreement upon which the claim is based.

Proceedings against mortgagors.

13–07.2 The additional requirements for particulars of claim where they relate to a mortgage of residential premises are set out in Pt 55. Details must be pleaded as to:
(1) whether a Class F land charge has been registered, or whether a notice under the Matrimonial Homes Act 1983 has been entered or whether a notice under the Family Law Act 1996 has been registered. If this is the case, the claimant must serve notice of the proceedings on any such person;
(2) the state of the mortgage account, including the amount of the advance, periodic payments and interest required, the amount needed to redeem the mortgage including solicitors' costs and administration charges and the rate of interest payable. If the mortgage is a regulated consumer credit agreement, they must state the total amount outstanding.

If the claim is based on arrears the particulars of claim must set out:
(3) in schedule form, the dates when the arrears arose, all amounts due, the dates and amounts of all payments made and a running total of the arrears;
(4) details of all other payments to be made and claimed;
(5) any relevant information about the defendant's circumstances, including details about benefits and payments direct; and
(6) any previous steps taken to recover arrears, with full details of any court proceedings.

Possession claims relating to mortgaged residential property.

13–07.3 CPR r.55.10 applies to such claims and requires that:
(1) the claimant must send a notice to the property addressed to "the occupiers" not less than 14 days before the hearing which must:
— state that a possession claim for the property has started;
— show the name and address of the claimant, the defendant and the court which issued the claim form; and
— give details of the hearing.
(2) The claimant must produce at the hearing a copy of the notice and evidence that he has served it.

Delete 13–C1 to 13–C3 and replace with:

13–C1 With the introduction of Pt 55, new forms have been designed. Under CPR PD55, para.1.5, the claimant must use the appropriate claim form and particulars of claim form set out in Table 1 to Pt 4 of the Practice Direction. The claim form must be in Form N5, N5B or N6 as appropriate. The particulars of claim form must be in Form N119, N120 or N121 as appropriate. The defence must be in Form N11, N11B, N11M or N11R as appropriate.

Section 17: Undue Influence

Classes of undue influence.

Add new footnote to end of second paragraph:

Note 1: The recent decision of *Nicholas Geoffrey Daniel v Irene Margaret Drew* [2005] EWCA Civ 507 gives useful guidance. See in particular para.31, where the Court of Appeal stated that: "In the broadest possible way, the difference between the two classes is that in the case of actual undue influence something has to be done to twist the mind of a donor whereas in cases of presumed undue influence it is more a case of what has not been done namely ensuring that independent advice is available to the donor."

17–03

Add at end of note 69:

For a modern example of a transaction between father and daughter where the presumption was held not to arise, see *Turkey v Awadh* [2005] EWCA Civ 382.

Add at end of note 77:

In *Mark Reginald Sutton v Mishcon De Reya* [2003] EWHC 3166; (2004) 1 F.L.R. 837, Ch, it was held that claims against the defendant law firms, alleging professional negligence in connection with a deed of cohabitation made between two parties in a master/slave sexual relationship, had no prospect of success. Hart J. found that there was no loss, as although there was nothing contrary to public policy in the deed, the deed was likely to be unenforceable in any event as it was difficult to suppose that it could ever have withstood an attack on one or more of the grounds of lack of intention to create legal relations, undue influence or misrepresentation.

Manifest disadvantage.

Add at end of second paragraph:

A recent example of the Court of Appeal correcting the application of the former, incorrect test can be found in *Macklin v Dowsett* [2004] EWCA Civ 904; [2004] 34 E.G. 68.

17–04

The effect of independent legal advice.

Add new footnote to end of first paragraph:

Note 1: Recent cases include *Joan Humphreys v Dennis Humphreys* [2004] EWHC 2201, Ch; *Stevens v Leeder (Aka Newey)* [2005] EWCA Civ 50.

17–05

Add at end of note 80:

Pesticchio v Huet was upheld on appeal: see [2004] EWCA Civ 372.

Position of third parties.

Add after second paragraph:

A replacement or substitute mortgage with the same lender would be voidable if it was inseparably connected with an earlier mortgage that was voidable for undue influence and of which the lender had constructive notice: see *Yorkshire Bank Plc v Pamela Tinsley* [2004] EWCA Civ 816; [2004] 3 All E.R. 463.

17–05A

Defences.

Add at end of second paragraph:

17–09.2 For a recent example of an unsuccessful attempt to plead undue influence as a defence see *Fladgate Fielder (A Firm) v Smith* [2005] All E.R. (D) 264 (May) where, on a summary judgment application, the court found that in order to establish a defence based on undue influence (in the absence of express undue influence), it was necessary to establish two pre-requisites, namely (1) a relationship of trust and confidence between the parties and (2) that the transaction called for an explanation. Warren J. held that there was no reasonable prospect of establishing the second pre-requisite.

Part D

BUSINESS LAW

Section 18: Introduction

Add after para.18–08:

"Distance selling"
Important changes have been made to the law of credit, financing and leasing and to the **18–08.1**
law of sale of goods by the introduction of EU rules as to distance selling. "Distance selling" includes any contract negotiated at a distance and includes letter, telephone call, mail order, fax, video text, teleshopping and all forms of "e-commerce". The principal changes are contained in the Consumer Protection (Distance Selling) Regulations (SI 2000/2334) and the Financial Services (Distance Marketing) Regulations 2004 (SI 2004/2095). Their effect will be noted in Sections 19 and 24 below.

Consumer credit
The Government is engaged in a wholesale review of the law of consumer credit, fol- **18–08.2**
lowing the publication of its White Paper *Fair, Clear and Competitive—The Consumer Credit Market in the 21st Century* (Cmnd. 6040) in December 2003. A new Consumer Credit Bill was almost through Parliament when it was lost by the dissolution in April 2005. The bill has been re-introduced in the new Parliament and may well have been passed by the time this Supplement is published. The changes it brings about are unlikely to take effect immediately and will be noted in future editions. In the meantime, substantial changes have already been achieved by:
- the Consumer Credit (Agreements) (Amendment) Regulations 2004 (SI 2004/1482);
- the Consumer Credit (Advertisements) Regulations (SI 2004/1484);
- the Consumer Credit (Enforcement, Default and Termination Notices) (Amendment) Regulations 2004 (SI 2004/3237);
- the Consumer Credit (Disclosure of Information) Regulations 2004 (SI 2004/1481);
- the Consumer Credit (Early Settlement) Regulations 2004 (SI 2004/1483).

Their effect will be noted in Section 19 below.

Section 19: Credit, Finance and Leasing

Statutory controls

Add at end:

19–03 Note that the Consumer Credit Bill, which was abandoned on the dissolution of Parliament, has been re-introduced and is likely to become law in 2005 (though its provisions will have a longer lead-in time). This will make major changes to the Consumer Credit Act 1974, including the redefinition of "consumer" and the abolition of the financial limits of control. Its effects will be noted in a future edition.

Add after para.19–12:

Distance selling

19–12.1 Credit and leasing agreements are affected by the Consumer Protection (Distance Selling) Regulations (SI 2000/2334) and the Financial Services (Distance Marketing) Regulations 2004 (SI 2004/2095). For "distance selling" see para.18–09, above.

These Regulations define "consumer" as a natural person who contracts for purposes which are outside his business. The 2000 Regulations apply to most types of sale of goods or services and require the supplier to provide the consumer with a lot of information (including notice of the right to cancel) both before and after the conclusion of the contract.

Regulation 10 of the 2000 Regulations gives the consumer a right of cancellation (subject to limited exceptions under reg.13) and if notice of cancellation is given, it is as if the contract had never been made. If the supplier has given all the requisite information, the consumer has seven days from the contract being concluded (or if the information is given post-contract) from the date the information was given. In all other cases the consumer has three months plus seven working days from delivery of the goods (supply of goods) or the conclusion of the contract (supply of services).

On cancellation, all sums paid by or on behalf of the consumer must be reimbursed and all security returned (reg.14) and any related credit agreement is automatically cancelled by the same notice (reg.15), again with sums reimbursed and security returned. Any credit paid to the consumer must be repaid (reg.16). Pending return of goods, the consumer must retain possession and take reasonable care of them (reg.17).

It should also be noticed that a consumer has the right to cancel payment where fraudulent use has been made of his payment card and has the right to be re-credited with the amount of the payment by the credit provider (reg.21).

The 2004 Regulations provide an analogous right of cancellation of credit agreements concluded at a distance.

The Consumer Credit Act 1974

Financial limits.

Add at end:

19–15 Note that if the Consumer Credit Bill introduced early in the new Parliament becomes law, the financial limits of control will be abolished.

Pre-contract.

Add at end:

19–18 As a result of the White Paper (see above), s.55 of the Consumer Credit Act (disclosure of information), which had lain dormant since 1974, has been activated and the Consumer

Credit (Disclosure of Information) Regulations 2004 (SI 2004/1481) came into force on May 31, 2005. Creditors and owners are obliged to give prospective customers in advance virtually all the information made obligatory for the agreement itself and in a document separate from the agreement itself. Non-compliance renders any subsequent agreement improperly executed and thus potentially unenforceable.

The formalities of the agreement.

Add at end:

19–19 Major changes have been made to the 1983 Agreements Regulations by the Consumer Credit (Agreements) (Amendment) Regulations 2004 (SI 2004/1482) which came into force on May 31, 2005 and apply to agreements made after that date. The major changes are:
    1. the prescribed information has now to be given in a fixed and immutable order;
    2. there are significant changes to the warning boxes and additional warning and consent boxes introduced;
    3. additional information has to be given;
    4. the legibility and prominence provisions have been made much stricter;
    5. changes have been made to the method of calculation and to the statement of the APR.

Practitioners confronted by an agreement made after May 31, 2005 must check the new Regulations to see that it conforms.

Extortionate credit bargains.

Add at end:

19–25 The re-introduction of the Consumer Credit Bill into Parliament means that this area of the 1974 Act will be drastically changed. The proposed new Act will create a new category of "unfair relationships" and will give the courts wide powers to rewrite consumer agreements if:
    1. the terms of the agreement are "unfair" to the debtor or hirer;
    2. the way in which the creditor or owner has exercised or enforced any of his rights is unfair;
    3. anything else done (or not done) by the creditor or owner, whether before, during or after the agreement, is unfair.

The old "extortionate credit bargain" provisions were little used and it is the Government's intention that the courts will be spurred by the new provisions to be a great deal more proactive.

Defences

Add at end:

19–43 The provisions relating to "distance selling" (see paras 18–09 and 19–12.1, above) afford new defences based on cancellation or deemed cancellation. A specimen form is included in this Supplement.

A. CLAIMS BY THE CREDITOR OR OWNER AGAINST THE DEBTOR OR HIRER

Hire-purchase and conditional sale agreements

19–D5 Note that new provisions for the sums payable on early termination were introduced by the Consumer Credit (Early Settlement) Regulations 2004 (SI 2004/1483) which came into force on May 31, 2005.

Credit tokens (regulated agreements)

Add at end:

19–D16 Credit cards: Under the Consumer Protection (Distance Selling) Regulations 2000 (SI 2000/2334), a consumer has the right to cancel payment where fraudulent use has been made of his payment card and has the right to be re-credited with the amount of the payment by the credit provider (reg.21).

Add at end:

19–D17 Credit cards: Under the Consumer Protection (Distance Selling) Regulations 2000 (SI 2000/2334), a consumer has the right to cancel payment where fraudulent use has been made of his payment card and has the right to be re-credited with the amount of the payment by the credit provider (reg.21).

I. DEFENCES AGAINST ACTIONS BY THE CREDITOR OR OWNER

Regulated agreements: making of the contract

Add at end:

19–D50 Note that major changes have been made to the 1983 Agreements Regulations by the Consumer Credit (Agreements) (Amendment) Regulations 2004 (SI 2004/1482) which came into force on May 31, 2005 and apply to agreements made after that date. See para.19–19, above.

Add at end:

19–D51 Note that major changes have been made to the 1983 Agreements Regulations by the Consumer Credit (Agreements) (Amendment) Regulations 2004 (SI 2004/1482) which came into force on May 31, 2005 and apply to agreements made after that date. See para.19–19 above.

Regulated agreements: events after the making of the contract

Add after 19–D58:

Defence in relation to a "distance selling" transaction   19–D58.1

To be inserted in s.4 of Form 9B or 9D or contained in a separate document

1. The Defendant admits that he entered into the agreement referred to in the Particulars of Claim ("the credit agreement").

2. The credit agreement was made in order to finance a contract between the Defendant and CD whereby CD sold [*specify goods*] to the Defendant at a price of £[   ] ("the sale agreement").

3. The sale agreement was a distance contract within the meaning of the Consumer Protection (Distance Selling) Regulations 2000 ("the 2000 Regulations") in that [*set out the circumstances relied on as showing that this was a distance contract*].

4. Under reg.10 of the 2000 Regulations, the Defendant had the right to cancel the sale agreement.

5. By a notice given [*date*] a copy of which is annexed to this Defence, the Defendant duly cancelled the sale agreement. Under reg.15 of the 2000 Regulations, the cancellation of the sale agreement operated automatically to cancel the credit agreement and the credit agreement ceased to be enforceable.

[*Alternatively*]

4. In breach of the sale agreement, CD failed to deliver the said goods within the date specified for delivery.

5. Under reg.20 of the 2000 Regulations, such failure operated in the same way as if the Defendant had given a valid notice of cancellation under reg.10.

The credit agreement was thereby automatically cancelled and ceased to be enforceable.

6. In the circumstances, the Defendant is not liable to the Claimant in the sum claimed or any sum.

Section 20: Commission Agents

Add after para.20–01.1:

For the 1993 Regulations to apply there must be a contractual relationship of principal **20–01.2**
and agent between the parties. A sub-agent who had not directly contracted with the principal could not invoke the Regulations—*Light v Ty Europe Ltd* [2004] 1 Lloyd's Rep 693.

The compensation provisions which apply on termination operate when the contract expires by effluxion of time—*Light v Ty Europe Ltd* (above); *Cooper v Pure Fishing Ltd* [2004] 2 Lloyd's Rep 518.

Section 24: Sale of Goods

Consumers, producers and guarantors

Add at end:

24–01.1 Note that the law in relation to the definition of "consumer" is now in some disarray. For the purposes of all legislation, apart from the Unfair Contract Terms Act 1977, a "consumer" must be a natural person. In a somewhat bizarre decision of the Court of Appeal, however, the court held that a limited company (indeed a public limited company) can be a "consumer" under s.12 of the 1977 Act—*Feldarol Foundry Plc v Hermes Leasing (London) Ltd* [2004] EWCA Civ 747. That case involved the acquisition on hire-purchase of a car for the use of the company's chairman and the court took the view that as acquiring cars was not the "business" of a steel foundry, the company had contracted as consumer. This remains, therefore, a pitfall for the unwary.

Add after para.24–09.1:

Distance selling

24–09.2 The law of sale of goods has been modified by the Consumer Protection (Distance Selling) Regulations (SI 2000/2334). For "distance selling" see para.18–09, above.

These Regulations define "consumer" as a natural person who contracts for purposes which outside his business. The 2000 Regulations apply to most types of sale of goods or services and require the supplier to provide the consumer with a lot of information (including notice of the right to cancel) both before and after the conclusion of the contract.

Regulation 10 of the 2000 Regulations gives the consumer a right of cancellation (subject to limited exceptions under reg.13) and if notice of cancellation is given, it is as if the contract had never been made. If the supplier has given all the requisite information, the consumer has seven days from the contract being concluded (or if the information is given post-contract) from the date the information was given. In all other cases the consumer has three months plus seven working days from delivery of the goods (supply of goods) or the conclusion of the contract (supply of services).

On cancellation, all sums paid by or on behalf of the consumer must be reimbursed and all security returned (reg.14) and any related credit agreement is automatically cancelled by the same notice (reg.15), again with sums reimbursed and security returned. Any credit paid to the consumer must be repaid (reg.16). Pending return of goods, the consumer must retain possession and take reasonable care of them (reg.17).

Note also that the 2000 Regulations also contain very drastic provisions against inertia selling.

Defences

Defences of the buyer

Add at end:

24–37.2 Note the problems with "consumer" under the Unfair Contract Terms Act 1977, noted under para.24–01, above.

Note also that the rules relating to "distance selling" will afford an additional line of defence in relevant cases—see para.24–09.2, above. A new precedent is added to exemplify this.

Buyer's Defences

Add after 24–D58:

24–D59   **Defence in relation to a "distance selling" transaction**

To be inserted in s.4 of Form 9B or 9D or contained in a separate document

1. The Defendant admits that he entered into the agreement referred to in the Particulars of Claim.

2. The agreement was a distance contract within the meaning of the Consumer Protection (Distance Selling) Regulations 2000 ("the 2000 Regulations") in that [*set out the circumstances relied on as showing that this was a distance contract*].

3. Under reg.10 of the 2000 Regulations, the Defendant had the right to cancel the agreement.

4. By a notice given [*date*] a copy of which is annexed to this Defence, the Defendant duly cancelled the agreement. Under reg.10(2) of the 2000 Regulations, the effect of such notice is that the agreement is to be treated as if it had never been made.

[*Alternatively*]

3. In breach of the agreement, the Claimant failed to deliver the said goods within the date specified for delivery.

4. Under reg.20 of the 2000 Regulations, such failure operated in the same way as if the Defendant had given a valid notice of cancellation under reg.10.

5. In the circumstances, the Defendant is not liable to the Claimant in the sum claimed or any sum.

Section 25: Title to Goods—Torts Against Goods

After para.25–16 add:

Inertia selling

25–17 The Consumer Protection (Distance Selling) Regulations 2000 (SI 2000/2334) have introduced fierce new rules in respect of inertia selling. Regulation 24 applies if unsolicited goods are send to a person with a view to his acquiring them, the recipient has no reasonable cause to believe they were sent to be acquired by the recipient's business and the recipient did not agree to acquire or return them. In those circumstances, the recipient is entitled to treat the goods as an unconditional gift to him and the sender's rights are extinguished. In certain circumstances, the sender is also guilty of a criminal offence.

A new precedent is added to exemplify this.

Miscellaneous Defences

Add after 25–D31:

Defence relying on "inertia selling" 25–D32

To be inserted in s.4 of Form 9B or 9D or contained in a separate document

1. The Defendant admits that he received the goods to which the claim relates from the Claimant.

2. The Defendant further admits that he has [retained] [sold] [destroyed] [refused to return] the goods but states that he was entitled to do so in the following circumstances.

3. When the goods were sent to the Defendant, they were unsolicited. The Defendant had not agreed to acquire or return the goods and had no reasonable cause to believe that they were sent with a view to their being acquired for the purposes of a business.

4. In the circumstances, the Claimant was guilty of inertia selling within the meaning of the Consumer Protection (Distance Selling) Regulations 2000 ("the 2000 Regulations").

5. Under reg.24(2) of the 2000 Regulations, the Defendant was entitled to use, deal with or dispose of the goods as if they were an unconditional gift to him and under reg.24(3), the rights of the Claimant to the goods were extinguished.

6. In the circumstances, the Claimant is not entitled to the relief claimed or to any relief.

Part E

COMPUTERS AND INFORMATION TECHNOLOGY

SECTION 27: COMPUTERS AND INFORMATION TECHNOLOGY

Breach of contract in relation to defects.

Add at end:

In *SAM Business Systems v Hedley* [2002] EWHC 2733; [2003] 1 All E.R. (Comm) 465, TCC, Judge Bowsher Q.C. said that a software system sold as a tried and tested system should not contain bugs.

27–04

Breach of contract in relation to time of performance and delay.

Add at end:

In *Peregrine Systems Ltd v Steria Ltd* [2005] EWCA Civ 239 at [15] it was held that the question whether a reasonable time has been exceeded requires a broad consideration, with the benefit of hindsight, and viewed from the time at which one party contends that a reasonable time for performance has been exceeded, of what would, in all the circumstances which are by then known to have happened, have been a reasonable time for performance.

27–05

Misrepresentations during negotiations.

Add at end:

The reasonableness of exclusion clauses in an IT contract was considered (after *Watford v Sanderson*) in *SAM Business Systems v Hedley* (above).

27–07

Damages.

Add at end:

A claim for wasted management time was rejected in *Peregrine Systems Ltd v Steria Ltd* [2004] EWHC 275, TCC, a case concerning an IT contract, on the ground that the evidence of the time which had been wasted was not satisfactory (the judgment in the Court of Appeal did not deal with this point: [2005] EWCA Civ 239). In *Standard Chartered Bank v Pakistan National Shipping Corp* [2001] EWCA Civ 55; [2001] 1 All E.R. (Comm) 822 at [48], a claim for wasted management time was rejected on the ground that it had not been proved that any loss had actually been incurred. See also *Carisbrooke Shipping CV5 v Bird Port Ltd* [2005] EWHC 1974 (Comm) at [154]–[171].

27–11

Part F

DEFAMATION

Section 28: Libel and Slander

Pleading the Particulars of Claim

Pleading foreign publication
Libel and slander.
Add to end of first sentence, after citation for Berezovsky v Forbes:

and *Don King v Lennox Lewis* [2005] E.M.L.R. 4   **28–21**

Remedies

Compensatory damages
Libel and slander.
Add at end, after citation for Rubber Improvement Ltd v Daily Telegraph Ltd:

and *Collins Stewart Ltd v Financial Times Ltd* [2005] EWHC 262, QB   **28–24**

Special damage
Libel and slander.
Add after first sentence:

An alleged shortfall in the market capitalisation of a company as a suggested measure of special damages is too uncertain to be acceptable as a legal basis for assessing damages (*Collins Stewart Ltd v Financial Times Ltd (No.1)* [2004] EWHC 2337, QB).   **28–26**

Injunction
Libel and slander.
In third and fourth lines, for "interlocutory", substitute:

interim   **28–27**

Add at end:

The rule in *Bonnard v Perryman* has recently been reaffirmed in *Greene v Associated Newspapers Ltd* [2004] EWCA Civ 1462.

Defences

Pleading an alternative meaning in a defence
Change citation for De L'Isle v Times Newspapers to:

[1988] 1 W.L.R. 49   **28–30**

Justification: Libel and slander
Generally.
In the eighth sentence (after the quote from from McPhilemy v Times Newspapers Limited) amend the words after the comma as follows:

i.e. what defamatory meaning he seeks to justify: see para.2.5(1) of CPR PD53.   **28–32**

Absolute privilege: libel and slander

Generally.

Add after the citation for Trapp v Mackie:

28–42   and *Gray v Avadis* [2003] EWHC 1830, QB

Qualified privilege: libel and slander

At common law: generally.

Add after the second sentence of last paragraph:

28–44   However in *Jameel v Wall Street Journal* [2005] EWCA Civ 74 the Court of Appeal held that the phrase "responsible journalism" was insufficiently precise to constitute the sole test for Reynolds privilege. They stated that "responsible journalism" denoted the degree of care a journalist should exercise before publishing a defamatory statement and added that a further element had to be demonstrated, namely that the subject-matter must be of such a nature that it is in the public interest that the defamatory publication should be published (note that this is more stringent than just that the public should be interested in receiving the information). This case is presently the subject of appeal to the House of Lords.

Add at end:

Further, in *Jameel*, the Court of Appeal emphasised that a defendant, relying on Reynolds privilege, should make clear where he is relying on "reasonable belief in the truth of matters published, or their implications, and where he is not". Equally, a claimant "should make clear whether he denies that the belief was held, or whether he merely contends that the belief was not reasonable.

Offer of amends: s.2 of the Defamation Act 1996

Libel and slander:

Add to end of penultimate sentence:

28–48   and the Court of Appeal guidance in *Nail v News Group Newspapers & Harper Collins* [2004] EWCA Civ 1708. For useful guidance as to the amounts and discounts likely to be awarded by the court after an offer of amends has been accepted, see the recent decisions of Eady J. in *Turner v News Group Newspapers Ltd* [2005] EWHC 892, QB and *Campbell-James v Guardian Media Group* [2005] EWHC 893, QB.

Replies

Pleading malice: libel and slander: fair comment and qualified privilege.

Add after the citation for Horrocks v Lowe:

28–55   For a recent analysis of the law on malice in the context of qualified privilege, see *Rackham v Sandy* [2005] EWHC 482.

Qualified privilege/fair comment.

Add at end:

28–56   or that the defendant did not hold the belief stated in the *Reynolds* defence alternatively that he did hold such a belief but that the belief was not reasonable (*Jameel v Wall Street Journal* [2005] EWCA Civ 74).

SUPPLEMENT 1—NOVEMBER, 2005

Rebutting a defence that an Offer to make Amends has been made.

Add after citation for Milne v Express Newspapers:

, upheld by the Court of Appeal: [2005] 1 W.L.R. 772   **28–57A**

Amend title:

Claim for damages for libel published on the Internet — Injunction

Replace paragraph 4. with:

4. At all material times the web-site was accessible to millions of users of the World Wide Web. The press release was published on the web-site from [date] to at least [date].   **28–F6**

Delete paragraphs 5. to 7.

SECTION 29: MALICIOUS FALSEHOOD

Mere puffing not actionable.

Add at end:

Moreover, in the case of *Charterhouse Clinical Research Unit Ltd v Richmond Pharmacology* [2003] EWHC 1099, QB, Morland J. held that the courts must keep claims alleging trade libels within their proper bounds, particularly having regard to s.12(4) of the Human Rights Act 1998 and Art.10 of the European Convention on Human Rights. **29–02A**

Part H

EMPLOYMENT

Section 31: Employment Tribunal

Proceedings in the Employment Tribunal

Replace paras 31–01 to 31–03.1 with:

The Employment Tribunals (Constitution and Rules of Procedure) Regulations 2004 (SI 2004/1861) have now replaced the 2001 Regulations. The 2004 Regulations came into force on October 1, 2004, and apply in Scotland as well as in England and Wales. Schedule 1 to the 2004 Regulations sets out the rules of procedure now to be adopted in the employment tribunal. **31–01**

Under those rules, prescribed information must now be included in a claim form (r.1(4)), response (r.4(3)) and counterclaim (r.7(1)). Similar provisions were made under the 2001 Rules, but were no more than directory.

A person bringing a claim after October 1, 2004 is known as a claimant, rather than an applicant. Two or more claimants may present their claims in the same document if their claims arise out of the same set of facts. Pursuant to r.1(4), the claim form must include the following information:

(a) each claimant's name;
(b) each claimant's address;
(c) the name of each person against whom the claim is made ("the respondent");
(d) each respondent's address;
(e) details of the claim;
(f) whether or not the claimant is or was an employee of the respondent;
(g) whether or not the claim includes a complaint that the respondent has dismissed the claimant or has contemplated doing so;
(h) whether or not the claimant has raised the subject matter of the claim with the respondent in writing at least 28 days prior to presenting the claim to an Employment Tribunal Office;
(i) if the claimant has not done as described in (h), why he has not done so.

References to dismissal in r.1(4) do not include reference to constructive dismissal. If the claimant is not or was not an employee of the respondent, the information referred to at (g)–(i) above is not required. If the claimant was an employee, but complains only of dismissal (or that the respondent has contemplated dismissal), the information referred to at (h)–(i) above is not required. If the claimant was an employee of the respondent and the claim does not relate to dismissal or contemplated dismissal, and the claimant has raised the subject matter of the claim as described at (h) above, the information referred to at (i) above is not required. **31–02**

Pursuant to r.4(3), a response (previously known as a notice of appearance) must include the following information:

(a) the respondent's full name;
(b) the respondent's address
(c) whether or not the respondent wishes to resist the claim in whole or in part; and
(d) if the respondent wishes to so resist, on what grounds.

A single document may include the response to more than one claim if the relief arises out of the same set of facts, provided that the respondent intends to resist all the claims on the same grounds, or does not intend to resist any of the claims. A single document may include the response of more than one respondent to a single claim, provided that each respondent intends to resist the claim on the same grounds, or none of the respondents intends to resist the claim.

Pursuant to r.7(1), a counterclaim brought in accordance with art.4 of the Employment Tribunals Extension of Jurisdiction (England and Wales) Order or art.4 of the Employ-

ment Tribunals Extension of Jurisdiction (Scotland) Order must include the following information:
- (a) the respondent's name;
- (b) the respondent's address;
- (c) the name of each claimant whom the counterclaim is made against;
- (d) the claimant's address;
- (e) details of the counterclaim.

31–03 Whereas prior to the 2004 Regulations, no particular form needed to be used for making or responding to a complaint to the tribunal, Sch.1 makes mandatory the use of prescribed forms for both claims and responses. Failure to use such forms will result in non-acceptance of the claim (r.3) or the response (r.6) by the Secretary to the tribunal. Use of the prescribed forms was due to become mandatory on April 1, 2005. That date has since been put back to October 1, 2005. The prescribed forms are available at *www.employmenttribunals.gov.uk*.

The statutory grievance, disciplinary and dismissal procedures have an important impact on when a claim should be brought. As will be seen below, in certain circumstances the tribunal will not accept the claim, or will usually reduce or increase the award otherwise payable to a claimant, in the event of non-compliance with such procedures.

A respondent now has 28 days from the date on which he was sent a copy of the claim to respond (r.4(1)). A default judgment may now be issued by a chairman if the response is not presented on time (r.8(1)).

31–03.1 Though an application to extend time for presentation of a response can be made (r.4(4)), such application must—unless an application is made under r.33(1) to review a default judgment—be made within 28 days of the claim being sent. The chairman shall only extend time for service if satisfied that it is just and equitable to do so.

In the event that a respondent fails to respond within the 28 day period, but no default judgment has been issued, an extension of time for responding to the claim may still be obtained. See *Moroak v Cromie* UKEAT/0093/05/DM. There, the EAT held that the tribunal had the power to review a decision not to admit a response in such circumstances. Guidance is also given in that case on the matters to be taken into account when deciding whether or not to admit a response out of time.

The Human Rights Act 1998.

Replace with:

31–03.2 As regards the overriding objective of the tribunals and chairmen to deal with cases justly, see now reg.3 of the 2004 Regulations.

The Employment Act 2002.

Replace with:

31–03.3 The Employment Bill 2001 has now been enacted as the Employment Act 2002 ("the 2002 Act"). Several of the provisions of the 2002 Act discussed below came into force on October 1, 2004. That date was also the commencement date of the Employment Act 2002 (Dispute Resolution) Regulations 2004 ("the EADR Regulations 2004").

It is beyond the scope of this work to include full details of the changes introduced by the 2002 Act and EADR Regulations 2004. Careful reference should be made to text of both, and to the new rules of procedure, to ensure compliance. Key provisions in the new Act and Regulations include the following:
- (a) Employers and employees must ordinarily comply with the statutory grievance, dismissal and disciplinary procedures set out in Sch.2 to the 2002 Act. (Employers can still follow their own procedures if these are additional to and not inconsistent with those required by statute.) For exceptions to the need to comply with the statutory procedures, see regs 4 and 11 of the EADR Regulations 2004. As to circumstances in which the parties are to be treated as complying with the statutory procedures, see regs 5 and 7.

(b) Use of an expedited modified grievance/dismissal/disciplinary procedure is permitted in particular prescribed cases. See regs 3(2) and 6(3) of the EADR Regulations 2004.
(c) At a date yet to be appointed, the statutory grievance, disciplinary and dismissal procedures will be implied by statute into all contracts of employment. See s.30 of the 2002 Act.
(d) Where in proceedings by an employee relating to a claim under any of the jurisdictions listed in Sch.3 to the 2002 Act, the standard statutory disciplinary/grievance procedure has not been completed then, save where there are exceptional circumstances which would make a reduction or increase of that percentage unjust or inequitable, the tribunal must (depending on the party in default) increase or decrease any award to the employee by between 10 and 50 per cent. See further s.31(3) and (4) of the 2002 Act.
(e) An employee shall not present a complaint to an employment tribunal under any of the jurisdictions listed in Sch.4 to the 2002 Act if it concerns a complaint about a grievance (*i.e.* "a complaint by an employee about action which his employer has taken or is contemplating taking in relation to him") and either (i) the grievance procedure (standard or modified) has not already been complied with; or (ii) less than 28 days have passed since the day of compliance; or (iii) compliance occurred more than one month after the original time limit for making the complaint. See further s.32 of the 2002 Act. Pursuant to s.32(6), a tribunal shall be prevented from considering such a complaint if breach of the provisions of s.32(2)–(4) is apparent to the tribunal from information supplied to it by the employee in connection with the bringing of the proceedings, or if the tribunal is satisfied of such breach as a result of the employer raising the issue of compliance.
(f) Failure to follow the appropriate disciplinary procedure in a dismissal claim will result in a dismissal being automatically unfair. See s.98A of the Employment Rights Act 1996, as enacted by s.34 of the 2002 Act.
(g) The normal time limit for lodging a complaint with the employment tribunal will, in certain cases, be extended by three months beginning with the day after the day on which it would otherwise have expired. See reg.15 of the EADR Regulations 2004.

Non pecuniary loss.

Delete the first three paragraphs and the quote and replace with:

The House of Lords has confirmed that a claimant may not recover under s.123(1) of the Employment Rights Act 1996 in respect of non-pecuniary loss such as injury to feelings in the context of a claim for unfair dismissal: see *Dunnachie v Kingston-upon-Hull City Council* [2004] I.R.L.R. 727. **31–03.4**

In what was the fourth paragraph, delete "Of course, assuming Dunnachie is not successfully appealed,".

Add after para.31–03.4:

A compromise agreement must, pursuant to s.203 of the Employment Rights Act 1996, "relate to the particular proceedings". As to how "particular" the contents must be, see *Hinton v University of East London* [2005] I.R.L.R. 552. There, Lady Justice Smith held "it is not sufficient to use a rolled-up approach such as 'all statutory rights'", and that particular or potential claims intended to be subject to the agreement ought to be identified "either by a generic description such as 'unfair dismissal' or by reference to the section of the statute giving rise to the claim." Lady Justice Smith also considered that use of "a standard form of compromise agreement which lists every form of employment right known to the law" would not constitute "good practise", and that "compromise agreements should be tailored to the individual circumstances of the instant case." **31–03.5**

Section 33: Industrial Action

Immunity

Add at end:

In so far as a trade dispute is defined (s.244 TULRCA) as a dispute which relates wholly or mainly to (a) terms and conditions of employment, the terms and conditions in question need not be those of the striking workers themselves, see *British Telecommunications Plc v Communications Workers Union* [2004] I.R.L.R. 58. **33–08**

Loss of immunity

Add at end of second paragraph:

TULRCA s.232B was amended with effect from April 6, 2005, so that the reference to s.230(2A) now reads s.230(2B). **33–10**

Replace paragraph (i) with:

(i) The employer must be notified of the action no less than seven days before the industrial action begins and given such information in the union's possession as would help the employer make plans and bring the information to the attention of those whom the union intends to induce to take part in the industrial action, and should be told whether the action is to be continuous or discontinuous and, if discontinuous, the intended dates of that action: TULRCA, s.234A(3). The information to be provided will include such information as the union possesses s to the number, category or workplace of the employees concerned but need not name them: s.234A(5A) and see *British Telecommunications Plc v Communications Workers Union* [2004] I.R.L.R. 58. This requirement is to be further prescribed by future amendment to s.234A(5A) pursuant to the Employment Relations Act 2004.

SECTION 34: TRADE UNIONS

Add after para.34–07:

Employment Relations Act 2004

34–08 The Employment Relations Act 2004 received the Royal Assent on September 16, 2004 and was brought fully into force by April 2005. Part 1 of the ERA 2004 amends the provisions of the TULR(C)A 1992 relating to the procedures for trade union recognition. Part 2 amends the provisions of the TULR(C)A 1992 relating to industrial action—see Section 33 above. Part 3 amends certain provisions of the TULR(C)A 1992 relating to the rights of trade union members (see further below) and other employment legislation (see Section 32 above). Part 5 amends the provisions of the TULR(C)A 1992 relating to the powers of the Certification Officer (see further below). Part 6 amends certain provisions of the TULR(C)A 1992 relating to trade union administration, funding and leadership elections.

In the context of the rights of trade union members with which this Section is concerned, the most important amendment introduced by the ERA 2004 is contained in s.33. This section amends ss.174–176 of the TULR(C)A 1992 dealing with exclusion or expulsion from trade unions on grounds of conduct. Section 33 was introduced to deal with the problem of members of fascist and far-right political parties joining trade unions with the intention of seeking compensation from the union if expelled for their political views. This had given rise to two unreported decisions of the Employment Appeal Tribunal: *ASLEF v Lee*, Febuary 24, 2004 and *Potter v UNISON*, March 1, 2004. In these two cases the EAT had held that although ss.174–176 of the TULR(C)A 1992 prohibited exclusion or expulsion on grounds of *membership* of a political party, it was permissible for a union to exclude or expel an individual who had engaged in political *activities* contrary to the aims and objectives of the union. Section 33 of the ERA 2004 formalises the approach of the EAT and takes it one stage further in relation to the availability of compensation.

Section 33 of the ERA 2004 amends ss.174–176 of the TULR(C)A 1992 by introducing a statutory distinction between "conduct which consists in the individual's being or ceasing to be, or having been or ceased to be, a member of a political party" on the one hand, and "conduct which consists of activities undertaken by an individual as a member of a political party" on the other. The former is "protected conduct", whereas the latter is not. An exclusion or expulsion wholly or mainly attributable to "protected conduct" is prohibited. This means that an exclusion or expulsion which is wholly or mainly attributable to an individual's *activities* as opposed to mere inactive *membership* of a political party is not prohibited. In addition, even if an exclusion or expulsion is mainly attributable to membership of a political party, but partly attributable to political activities, the individual in question is not entitled to a minimum award of compensation. Such an individual can only recover his or her actual loss which is unlikely to be significant.

The other significant amendment in relation to the rights of trade union members is that contained in s.48 of the ERA 2004. This section amends the TULR(C)A 1992 by providing the Certification Officer with power to strike out complaints which are scandalous, vexatious, have no reasonable prospect of success, or are otherwise misconceived. This is an important change which will allow the Certification Officer to dispose summarily of vexatious or groundless complaints made by trade union members.

SECTION 35: DISCRIMINATION IN EMPLOYMENT

Originating Applications.

Add at end:

See now the Employment Tribunals (Constitution and Rules of Procedure) Regulations 2004 (SI 2004/1861), described and explained at para.31–01, above. **35–01.1**

Add at end:

Where a claim under the Equal Pay Act 1970 is made in respect of pregnancy or maternity related pay discrimination, then the comparator provisions of the Equal Pay Act 1970 are to be disregarded (*Alabaster v Barclays Bank Plc (formerly Woolwich Plc)* [2005] I.C.R. 1246; [2005] I.R.L.R. 576). Accordingly, though an actual comparator is usually required for a claim under the Equal Pay Act 1970, this is now not so in the case of a pregnancy or maternity related claim. **35–01.2**

Amendments.

Add at end:

See now the Employment Tribunals (Constitution and Rules of Procedure) Regulations 2004 (SI 2004/1861), described and explained at para.31–01, above. **35–03**

Questionnaire.

Add at end:

As to the drawing of inferences from a failure to reply to a questionnaire, s.65(2)(b) of the Race Relations Act 1976 (RRA) provides that where it appears to a tribunal that the respondent deliberately, and without reasonable excuse, omitted to reply within a reasonable period or that his reply is evasive or equivocal, the tribunal may draw any inference from that fact that it considers it just and equitable to draw, including an inference that he committed an unlawful act. This is so, however, only where the question relates to discrimination otherwise than on the grounds of race or ethnic or national origins. Where the question relates to discrimination on grounds of race or ethnic or national origins, or to harassment, the RRA now provides that such an inference may only be drawn where the respondent has failed to reply within eight weeks beginning with the day on which the question was served on him (s.65(2)(b), as amended by SI 2003/1626). The Disability Discrimination Act 1995 now also makes materially the same provision (s.56(3)). This brings them into line with the provision made in the Employment Equality (Religion or Belief) Regulations 2003 and the Employment Equality (Sexual Orientation) Regulations 2003 (reg.33) but, in the case of race discrimination, only in the case of discrimination related to race or ethnic or national origins, or to harassment, but not discrimination related to colour or nationality. This anomaly arises because the amendments made to s.65(2)(b) were effected by Regulations made under the s.2 of the European Communities Act 1972 made to give effect to the European Council Directive 2000/43/EC ("the Race Directive") which does not (in terms) address discrimination connected to colour and expressly excludes "nationality" from its scope (Art.3(2)). Similar anomalies arise elsewhere in the RRA for the same reason (see, *e.g.* ss.1(1A) and 3A RRA). This is unlikely to prove difficult in claims relating to discrimination connected to "colour" because such claims can easily be characterised as "race" discrimination also. However, the distinction may prove important in "nationality" related claims. **35–04**

For the importance of the questionnaire procedure to the discharging of the burden of proof, see *Igen Ltd (formerly Leeds Careers Guidance) v Wong* [2005] I.C.R. 931; [2005] I.R.L.R. 258.

Part J

ENVIRONMENTAL CLAIMS

Section 37: Introduction

Venue.

In second line of note 1, for "17th ed.", substitute:

18th ed.

In lines 7 and 8, for "Part 2E, pp. 361ff", substitute:

Part 2C, pp.290ff

Add at end:

Note that a revised TCC Court Guide is scheduled to come out on October 3, 2005. The most significant changes to the earlier edition of the Guide are fuller and more comprehensive Pre-Action Protocol requirements. Principal amongst the latter is the need for a letter of claim to be issued prior to proceedings being issued, with the need for a "defence" in some detail to be signalled to the other side, including any challenges to jurisdiction to be set out. Note too the Lord Chief Justice's Note of June 7, 2005 concerning a greater role for High Court participation and supervision in the TCC.

Group Actions.

In the third line, for "Pt 19B", substitute:

Pt 19PD

Replace first sentence of second paragraph with:

The courts have started to grapple with many of the problematic issues that arise with group litigation as opposed to individual cases proceeding separately. It is important for litigants to a Group Litigation Order to consider fully all aspects of the form of proceedings that group litigation entails. These issues include (i) deadlines for registration of claimants; (ii) the likelihood of the courts extending the deadline; (iii) generic and individual costs orders concerning group litigation claimants; and (iv) making and structuring Pt 36 payments into court.

There are also difficult third party liability issues arising. For example, on an application for indemnity and/or statutory contribution, to what extent is a third party bound by any settlement in respect of which he is asked to pay an indemnity or make a contribution. In *AB v British Coal Corporation* [2004] EWHC 1372, QB, the High Court held that a third party was bound by the settlement agreement, including because (i) the settlement had been endorsed by the courts (twice in fact) and (ii) the reasonableness of entering into the settlement, nor as to the terms overall, nor as to terms generically were challenged. This is an area where third parties as well as litigants in the main group litigation need to take care to ensure that all potential parties are notified of the litigation and of settlement terms.

Add after second sentence of second paragraph:

The courts have become more adept at addressing the risks of uncontrollable costs arising in group litigation, and have been innovative in using the CPR powers, for example, to address costs capping at an early stage of proceedings—see, for example, *Various Ledway Claimants v Kent and Medway Health Authority* [2003] EWHC 2551; [2003] All E.R. (D) 12 (Nov), QB.

Add at end of second paragraph:

See also *Chagos Islanders v Attorney General* [2003] EWHC 2222, QB and *AB v Leeds Teaching Hospital NHS Trust* [2004] EWHC 644; [2004] 2 F.L.R. 365, QB.

Add at end of third paragraph:

If a claimant intends to discontinue their claim, either in whole or in part, it is important that such intention is communicated clearly. Even if a claimant has so indicated, it is possible that a court will subsequently allow that claimant to withdraw the discontinuance—see *Re MMR and MR Vaccine Litigation (No.12); Sayers v Smithkline Beecham Plc* [2005] EWHC 539; [2005] All E.R. (D) 60 (Apr), QB. It is not clear, however, what principles the court will apply in determining whether to allow withdrawal of a notice of discontinuance. Furthermore, the courts have indicated that where a Group Litigation Order (albeit pre-CPR) was instituted by way of a Practice Direction of the Lord Chief Justice, it was not within the inherent powers of the court to regulate its own procedure to revoke the Group Litigation Order without the permission of the Lord Chief Justice—see *Re MMR and MR Vaccine Litigation (No.11)* [2004] EWHC 1899, QB. See also the latter case for an example where the court has doubted whether, even if a Group Litigation Order were revoked, the courts would allow the then individual cases to be continued separately (for example, because of the risk of inconsistent rulings). However, see in this context the refusal to allow a claimant to join a GLO, but granting permission to him to pursue his claim individually: *Taylor v Nugent Care Society* [2004] 1 W.L.R. 1129, CA.

Requirement for damage to be suffered.

Add after third sentence of second paragraph:

37–04 There is a suggestion that the test for a *quia timet* injunction in environmental cases of trespass, at least, is the higher "imminent danger of very substantial damage"—see *Drury v Secretary of State for the Environment, Food and Rural Affairs* [2004] 2 All E.R. 1056; [2004] 1 W.L.R. 1906.

Section 38: Nuisance

Delete footnote 2. It transpires from the Court of Appeal's ruling on appeal from the first **38–01**
instance case that the judge had applied as a cause of action ignis suus when no such action had been pleaded or argued before him—see Re-Source America International Ltd v Platt Site Services Ltd (Barkin Construction Ltd, Part 20 defendant) 95 Con.L.R. 1.

Add new footnote to end of second paragraph:
Note 1: Note that *Harrow London Borough Council v Qazi* is to be found at [2004] 1 A.C. 983.

Reasonable user.

Add at beginning:

This whole section may need to be re-thought in the light of the House of Lords ruling **38–02** in *Transco Plc v Stockport Metropolitan Borough Council* [2004] 2 A.C. 1. Although that case was addressed to *Rylands v Fletcher*, given the commonality of the origin of that cause of action with nuisance, the doubts expressed by the House of Lords there as to the applicability of a test of "reasonable user" are very likely to carry substantial weight with a court in a nuisance case. The House of Lords preferred the test of "ordinary user". See also Section 39 generally.

In first sentence of first paragraph, for "Ellison v Ministry of Defence 81 B.L.R. 101", substitute:

Arscott v Coal Authority [2004] EWCA Civ 892 (also of interest because a modern case applying the defence to a nuisance claim of protection against "the common enemy")

Add new footnote to end of last paragraph:
Note 1: Note that the *Marcic* case has been decided by the House of Lords (report at *Marcic v Thames Water Utilities Ltd* [2004] 1 All E.R. 135; [2004] B.L.R. 1; 91 Con.L.R. 1), and was against any cause of action in nuisance or for damages for breach of ECHR Art.8 rights where a sewerage undertaker was complying with its statutory duty and was not negligent as to its discharge.

Character of neighbourhood.

Add to end of second sentence:

and also to restrictive covenants—see *Hughes v Riley* [2005] All E.R. (D) 40 (Jul). **38–03**

Standard of comfort.

Add after first sentence:

The relevance of the concept of "abnormal sensitivity" in modern nuisance was seri- **38–04** ously doubted, but the cases cited in the previous sentence not expressly overruled, in *Network Rail Infrastructure Limited (t/a Railtrack Plc) v CJ Morris (t/a Soundstar Studio)* [2004] EWCA Civ 172. Given the strength of the disavowal it may well be more sensible to consider that this is no longer a pertinent concept paid heed by the courts.

Reasonable care.

Add at end of note 5:

38–05   This approach has found substantial favour with the Court of Appeal—see *Network Rail Infrastructure Limited (t/a Railtrack Plc) v CJ Morris (t/a Soundstar Studio)* [2004] EWCA Civ 172, where it was said of this *dictum* (para.32, *per* Buxton L.J.): "This very broad approach is thus firmly established as the essential content of liability in the modern law of nuisance, at least where the existence of a 'nuisance' is established. It takes the place of some detailed and particular rules that are to be found in earlier authority." However, this approach would not seem to apply to cases where the defence of statutory authority is in play—see *Marcic v Thames Water Utilities Ltd* [2004] 1 All E.R. 135; [2004] B.L.R. 1; 91 Con.L.R. 1. It may also be considered to apply, but perhaps be limited to cases where a "reasonableness" element is applicable, such as "adopting" or "continuing" a nuisance commenced by another—see *Transco Plc v Stockport MBC* [2004] 2 A.C. 1 at para.96, *per* Lord Walker.

Add after fourth paragraph:

Reasonable care is relevant generally to cases of adopting or continuing a nuisance—see *Transco Plc v Stockport MBC* [2004] 2 A.C. 1 at para.96, *per* Lord Walker.

Add at end:

It must be noted though, that the assimilation of at least *Rylands v Fletcher* to negligence, as had been suggested in Australia, was rejected by the House of Lords in *Transco Plc v Stockport Metropolitan Borough Council* [2004] 2 A.C. 1.

Statutory authority.

Replace third paragraph with:

38–06   In *Marcic v Thames Water Utilities Ltd* [2004] 1 All E.R. 135; [2004] B.L.R. 1; 91 Con.L.R. 1, the House of Lords upheld arguments, rejected by the Court of Appeal, that there could be no claim in nuisance where a sewerage undertaker was charged by statute to provide a service, necessarily limited as to extent and degree by statute-based financing rules applicable to the undertaker. Due to the fact that the pricing scheme was devised by statute, and that there was nothing to indicate that Parliament had required the defendant to bear an excessive burden as compared with the interests of the community, there could in such circumstances be no claim under Art.8 ECHR either.

Relevant type of damage.

Add after first sentence:

38–08   The concept or reasonable foreseeability of damage really "concerns ... not that of foreseeability alone, but of foreseeability as an aspect of reasonableness"—see *Network Rail Infrastructure Ltd (t/a Railtrack Plc) v CJ Morris (t/a Soundstar Studio)* [2004] EWCA Civ 172—and thus encompasses also aspects of remoteness (para.33, *per* Buxton L.J.).

Causal effect.

Add after first sentence:

38–09   Thus they must have "materially contributed" to the damage alleged to have been suffered—see *Brigham v London Borough of Ealing* [2003] EWCA Civ 1490 (citing the *Paterson* ruling with approval).

Private Nuisance

Instances of private nuisance.

Add to end of point 6.:

including by such diminution of a right to light as to cause a nuisance—see *Midtown Ltd v City of London Real Property Co Ltd; Joseph v City of London Real Property Co Ltd* [2005] All E.R. (D) 164 (Jan). **38–10**

Acts intending to annoy.

Add at end:

It is unclear whether an intentional act designed to cause distress would allow for damages for distress, which damages are otherwise irrecoverable. Such a cause of action and damages recoverable may be actionable for breach of privacy, and it is unclear whether the analogous case would also apply to nuisance—see *Wainwright v Home Office* [2004] 2 A.C. 406; [2003] 4 All E.R. 969. **38–11**

Who may sue (private nuisance).

Add after first sentence:

Note *Harrow London Borough Council v Qazi* [2004] 1 A.C. 983, where a person holding over after termination of a tenancy was held to be allowed to sue to protect Art.8 ECHR rights as regards protection of rights to his "home". It is unclear what effect this case will have as regards nuisance actions as the court held that Art.8 did not secure proprietary rights or contractual rights to possession. It would seem from this case though that no nuisance action will attach where there is no proprietary interest, but Art.8 may still protect from the effects of an alleged nuisance provided the effects are such as to reach the high threshold for engagement of Art.8 rights in this regard (see also *Khatun v United Kingdom* (above)). **38–12**

Add at end of second paragraph:

It has been doubted whether a claimed easement of support was a sufficient proprietary interest to enable damages to be recovered for interferance with it under *Rylands v Fletcher* (but the relevant considerations as regards claims in private nuisance are not likely to be different for these purposes)—see *Transco Plc v Stockport Metropolitan Borough Council* [2004] 2 A.C. 1. This may be important as linking sufficiency of a cause of action to the damages claimed, and leaves open the extent to which all "damages" which are reasonably foreseeable may be recoverable if not linked to the proprietary interest at stake.

Damages.

Add at end of third paragraph:

The House of Lords case *Transco Plc v Stockport Metropolitan Borough Council* [2004] 2 A.C. 1 suggests further that there is a necessary link as to recoverability of given damages to the proprietary interest in issue, and as with suggestion in *Hunter v Canary Wharf* (above), not all "damages" which are reasonably foreseeable may be recoverable if not linked to the proprietary interest at stake. **38–14.1**

Public nuisance.

Add at end of third paragraph:

and see also *Mistry v Thakor* [2005] All E.R. (D) 56 (Jul). **38–17**

SECTION 39: RYLANDS V FLETCHER

Liability under Rylands v Fletcher.

Insert before last sentence:

Such a view would correspond to the House of Lords ruling in *Transco Plc (formerly BG Plc and BG Transco Plc) v Stockport Metropolitan Borough Council* [2004] 1 All E.R. 589; 91 Con.L.R. 28. The court there considered that the preferred term should be "ordinary user", and also that the threshold for liability should be high, limited to matters of exceptional risk.

39–02

Strict Liability.

Add to end of penultimate sentence:

, and see also *Transco Plc (formerly BG Plc and BG Transco Plc) v Stockport MBC* [2004] 1 All E.R. 589; 91 Con.L.R. 28. However, note that the circumstances for liability arising in this cause of action has been revised by this case—see below.

39–03

Delete last sentence.

Escape.

Add after first sentence:

The House of Lords has affirmed the need in this cause of action for an escape "from one tenement to another": *Transco Plc (formerly BG Plc and BG Transco Plc) v Stockport MBC* [2004] 1 All E.R. 589; 91 Con.L.R. 28.

39–04

Non-natural user.

Add at end:

The statements in the previous paragraph do not seem to have been specifically overruled but are to be doubted as regards the future application of the cause of action of *Rylands v Fletcher*—see *Transco Plc (formerly BG Plc and BG Transco Plc) v Stockport MBC* [2004] 1 All E.R. 589; 91 Con.L.R. 28. The House of Lords doubted whether the concept of "non-natural user" was of any benefit, preferred the term "ordinary user" (doubted the benefit of references to "reasonable user") and considered that the question was "whether the defendant has done something which he recognises, or ought to recognise, as being quite out of the ordinary in the place and at the time when he does it" (*per* Lord Bingham). In this context Lord Bingham also considered that "little help is gained (and unnecessary confusion perhaps caused) by considering whether the use is proper for the general benefit of the community". Thus, those cases that considered the latter element as a necessary part of the defence are to be doubted as supplying a specific element of the cause of action (or defence). The specific defence accepted in *Ellison v Ministry of Defence* (above) may well be doubted in the light of *Transco*.

39–05

Section 40: Trespass

What is trespass?

Add at end of first paragraph:

40–01 , or if a defendant interferes with a claimant's air space that amounted to trespass except that that conduct would not constitute trespass if the interference were at such great height that it did not interfere with the claimant's airspace— *Laiqat v Majid* [2005] All E.R. (D) 231 (Jun).

Part L

FRAUD

SECTION 49: FRAUDULENT MISREPRESENTATION OR DECEIT

The representation.

Add at end:

The court will examine whether a subsequent statement made to the claimant or information provided to him is sufficiently complete to correct the misrepresentation (*Morris v Jones* [2002] EWCA Civ 1790).   **49–02**

Damage.

Add at end:

In assessing the measure of his loss, a claimant will also be required to give credit for any benefit received from the fraud (*Midco Holdings v Piper* [2004] EWCA Civ 476).   **49–05**

Frauds by agents.

Add at end:

The knowledge of a subordinate employee or agent of the falsity of the representations fixes a corporate defendant with vicarious liability as principal where the representations were made with the actual or ostensible authority of the defendant. Primary liability of the defendant may be alleged where the individuals constituting the "directing will and mind" of the corporate entity knew (or were reckless as to) the falsity of the representations that were innocently made on the company's behalf by other, more subordinate employees or agents. For a discussion of the pleading of the two different allegations, see *Enron (Thrace) Exploration and Production BV v Clapp (No.2)* [2005] EWHC 401.   **49–07**

On the attribution to a company of the knowledge of its agent for the purposes of s.213 of the Insolvency Act 1986 (liability for fraudulent trading), see *Bank of India v Christopher Morris* [2005] EWCA Civ 693.

SECTION 50: CONSPIRACY

Combination or agreement.

Add at end:

See also *Customs & Excise Commissioners v Total Network SL* (LTL 14/1/2005, **50–02**
unreported elsewhere) in which *Kuwait Oil Tanker CO SAK v Al Bader* [2000] 2 All E.R.
(Comm) 271, CA was applied.

Intention to injure.

Add at end:

In the case of *Michael Douglas v Hello! Ltd* [2005] EWCA Civ 595, the Court of Ap- **50–03**
peal conducted a useful review of the case law. The Lord Justices held that in all cases of
alleged unlawful interference with economic interests and unlawful means conspiracy in
which liability had been established, the necessary object or purpose of causing the claimant economic harm would not be considered to have been made out unless the conduct
could be shown to have been aimed or directed at the claimant, applying *Lonrho v Shell
Petroleum Co. Ltd* [1982] A.C. 173 and *Lonrho Plc v Fayed* [1991] 3 W.L.R. 188. The
Court of Appeal also held that foresight of the probable consequences or subjective
recklessness do not suffice as the mental element of the torts of economic loss, what is
required is intentional infliction of economic harm (see Lord Phillips M.R. at para.223:
"… it must be shown that the object or purpose of the defendant is to inflict harm on the
claimant, either as an end in itself, or as a means to another end. If foresight of the probable consequences or subjective recklessness sufficed as the mental element of the tort,
this would transform the nature of the tort").

Section 51: Inducing Breach of Contract and Unlawful Interference

Unlawful interference with trade or business

Intention to injure.

Add at end:

In the case of *Michael Douglas v Hello! Ltd* [2005] EWCA Civ 595, the Court of Appeal held that foresight of the probable consequences or subjective recklessness do not suffice as the mental element of the torts of economic loss, what is required is intentional infliction of economic harm. Lord Phillips M.R. held, at para.223, that: **51–12**

"... it must be shown that the object or purpose of the defendant is to inflict harm on the claimant, either as an end in itself, or as a means to another end. If foresight of the probable consequences or subjective recklessness sufficed as the mental element of the tort, this would transform the nature of the tort."

Section 52: Bribery

Remedies.

In the sixth line, for "(16th ed., London, 1996)", substitute:

(17th ed., London, 2001) **52–04**

Add at end:

In a recent bribery case, *Daraydan Holdings v Solland* [2004] EWHC 622, Ch, Lawrence Collins J. awarded the restitutionary remedy, applying *Att.-Gen. for Hong Kong v Reid*, and distinguishing the earlier House of Lords case of *Lister v Stubbs* (1890) L.R. 45.

Section 53: Constructive Trust and Tracing

Defences.

Add after second sentence in second paragraph:

Knowledge was imputed in *Crown Dilmun v Sutton* [2004] 1 B.C.L.C. 468, where the court reviewed relevant principles and authorities. **53–06**

Tracing.

Add to second paragraph, after citation for Re Hallett's Estate:

In *Boscawen and Bajwa* [1996] 1 W.L.R. 328 at 334–335 Millett L.J. treated every case in which a claimant traced his property into the hands of the defendant as one in which the court would treat the defendant as holding the property on a constructive trust. **53–07**

Add at end of first paragraph:

In *Compagnie Noga D'importation et D'Exportation SA v Australia and New Zealand Banking Group* [2005] EWHC 225, Langley J. expressed the view that it was a "nice question" as to whether, where property has passed through a purchaser, a claimant must make an allegation of bad faith or whether he may wait to see if good faith is asserted in a defence. **53–07.1**

Add at end:

In *Sinclair Investment Holdings SA v Versailles Trade Finance Ltd* [2004] All E.R. (D) 158, Nicholas Strauss Q.C., sitting as a deputy, declined to strike out a claim seeking to impose a constructive trust on the profits resulting from fraudulent transactions. The circumstances made it impossible for the claimant to trace or follow its funds but the judge permitted a constructive trust claim to proceed. He held that where a defendant has been party to the fraudulent misuse of the claimant's funds in such a way as to enable him to profit from illegitimate share dealings, it was at least arguable that the law should impose a trust.

Part M

HARASSMENT

Section 54: Harassment

Protection from Harassment Act 1997.

Add at end:

Section 1 of the Protection from Harassment Act 1997 requires that a claimant prove that an alleged harasser pursued a course of conduct amounting to harassment and which he knew or ought to have known amounted to harassment, having regard to whether a reasonable person in possession of the same information would think the course of conduct amounted to harassment. Thus the conduct, which includes speech, must be intentional and such as to harass the other individual, but in deciding what the alleged harasser knew or ought to have known at the relevant time, on the basis of the information available to him, the court applies an objective standard. Misconduct on one occasion will not suffice. In accordance with s.7(3), a course of conduct must involve conduct on at least two occasions and it is clear that the same person must be the victim on each occasion when harassment is alleged to have occurred: *Banks v Ablex Ltd* [2005] I.C.R. 819; [2005] I.R.L.R. 357. **54–02.1**

Add at end:

Employers may be vicariously liable under s.3 of the Protection from Harassment Act 1997 for their employees' acts of harassment of third parties, including fellow employees, committed in the course of employment, though the Act does not expressly provide for vicarious liability (*Majrowski v Guy's and St Thomas' NHS Trust* [2005] I.C.R. 977; [2005] I.R.L.R. 340). **54–02.2**

The Protection from Harassment Act 1997 may be used to bring claims in respect of harassment at work: *Majrowski v Guy's and St Thomas' NHS Trust* [2005] I.C.R. 977; [2005] I.R.L.R. 340; *Banks v Ablex Ltd* [2005] I.C.R. 819; [2005] I.R.L.R. 357.

Race, Sex and Disability Discrimination.

Add at end:

The Disability Discrimination Act 1995 now also addresses harassment expressly. A new s.3B (inserted by the Disability Discrimination Act 1995 (Amendment) Regulations 2003 (SI 2003/1673), made to implement Council Directive 2000/78/EC) defines harassment in materially the same terms as s.3A(1) RRA, set out at para.54–03.3, below. In addition, the Employment Equality (Religion or Belief) Regulations 2003 and the Employment Equality (Sexual Orientation) Regulations 2003 (made, again, to give effect to Council Directive 2000/78/EC) both define harassment similarly (reg.5). The harassment provisions in the DDA and in these Regulations apply only to harassment in the employment and related fields. **54–03**

Part O

IMMIGRATION

Section 57: Immigration

Add at end of first paragraph:

The recent Asylum and Immigration (Treatment of Claimants, etc) Act 2004 ("the 2004 Act") introduced substantial changes in the field of immigration and asylum law. Those changes include new provisions dealing with immigration offences, the treatment of claimants, enforcement powers, unification of the immigration appeal system into a single tier of appeal with limited onward review or appeal and certification on "safe third country" grounds. Earlier legislation referred to in this chapter should be read with the amendments introduced by the 2004 Act.

57–01

In the third paragraph, for "an immigration adjudicator", substitute:

the Asylum and Immigration Tribunal

57–02

In the fourth paragraph, for "an immigration adjudicator", sbustitute:

the Asylum and Immigration Tribunal

And for "Asylum and Immigration Appeals (Procedure) Rules SI 2003/652, r.7", substitute:

Asylum and Immigration Tribunal (Procedure) Rules 2005 (SI 2005/230), r.7

Replace the fifth paragraph with:

A party to an appeal to the Tribunal may apply to the appropriate court, on a point of law, for an order requiring the Tribunal to reconsider its decision: s.103A(1) of the 2002 Act. The time-limit for making an application for reconsideration is five days from service of the Tribunal's decision for an in country appeal or 28 days for an out of country appeal: s.103A(3) of the 2002 Act. Applications should be made to the appropriate court, which in England and Wales is the High Court: s.103A(9) of the 2002 Act. However, under transitional provisions applications should be made to the Tribunal at first instance, with a right to renew the application before the appropriate court within five days of service of the Tribunal's decision on the application: Sch.2, para.30 of the 2004 Act. The application is determined by reference only to written submissions and the determination is final: s.103A of the 2002 Act. The appropriate court may order the Tribunal to reconsider its decision or may refer the appeal to the appropriate appellate court (which in England and Wales is the Court of Appeal) if the question of law is one of importance: ss.103A(1), 103B(5) and 103C(1) of the 2002 Act. There is no right to apply for reconsideration if the jurisdiction of the Tribunal was exercised by three or more legally qualified members or if the hearing was one at which the Tribunal reconsidered its decision: ss.103A(8) and 103A(2)(b) of the 2002 Act. Instead, a party may appeal on a point of law, with permission, to the appropriate appellate court: ss.103B and 103E of the 2002 Act.

In the sixth paragraph, for "unless he has entry clearance or a work permit: s.92 of the 2002 Act", substitute:

unless he has entry clearance or a work permit, is in the United Kingdom at the time of refusal and certain other conditions are met: see s.92 of the 2002 Act, as amended by the 2004 Act.

In the second paragraph, for "an immigration adjudicator" substitute:

the Asylum and Immigration Tribunal

57–03.1

In the third paragraph, for "s.11 of the 1999 Act (removal under standing arrangements (namely the Dublin Convention) with other E.C. Member States) or under s.12 (removal to an E.C. Member State otherwise than under standing arrangements)", substitute:

Pts 2 to 5, Sch.3 of the 2004 Act

And for the penultimate sentence substitute:

The right of appeal in relation to a human rights claim may be exercised from within the United Kingdom unless the Secretary of State issues a "clearly unfounded" certificate under s.94 of the 2002 Act or Pts 2 to 5, Sch.3 of the 2004 Act.

Replace the fourth paragraph with:

The provisions relating to time limits for an appeal to the Tribunal in an asylum case, and relating to applications for reconsideration and appeals to the Tribunal, the High Court and the Court of Appeal on a point of law, are set out in ss.103A to 103E of the 2002 Act and in the Asylum and Immigration Tribunal (Procedure) Rules 2005: see above.

SUPPLEMENT 1—NOVEMBER, 2005

For Form N1 substitute Form AIT-1:

57–04

ASYLUM AND IMMIGRATION (TREATMENT OF CLAIMANTS, ETC.) ACT 2004

Notice of appeal to the Asylum and Immigration Tribunal (United Kingdom)

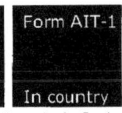

Form AIT-1

In country

Complete this form if you want to appeal from **inside** the United Kingdom and you have the right to do so.

If you want to appeal from **outside** the United Kingdom, you must use:
- appeal form AIT-2 if you are appealing against an Entry Clearance Officer's decision
- or appeal form AIT-3 if your right of appeal can only be exercised after having left the United Kingdom or you have chosen to leave the United Kingdom before exercising your right of appeal.

- To complete this appeal form, **please refer to the Information leaflet** that was sent to you with your notice of decision and this form. You can also find the leaflet on www.ait.gov.uk.
- Please complete this form in English. It is in your interest to complete this form as thoroughly as possible, and state all of your grounds in order for your appeal to be dealt with efficiently.
- Please complete Section 1 of this form by referring to the notice of decision that was sent to you by the Home Office.
- Where there is a check box ☐, put a check (X) in it to show your answer.
- You should send your notice of decision with this form. If you do not send the notice of decision with your appeal form, you must give your reasons in Section 8.

Section 1

A Home Office reference number

B Case Outcome ID

C Type of Decision

D Date of Service

E Deadline to appeal

F Method of Service

Your decision

Non-asylum ☐   Asylum ☐

/   /

/   /

Post ☐   Fax or Personal Service ☐

Section 2

The deadline to appeal is:
- **5 business days** from the date you were served with the decision, if you are detained under the Immigration Acts.
- **10 business days** from the date you were served with the decision, if you are not detained under the Immigration Acts.

Your appeal must be received by the Tribunal by the end of this period.

If you know your appeal is late, **or** if you are not sure your appeal will be received by the deadline date, **you must apply for an extension of time, and give your reasons for failing to submit your appeal in time, in the box →**

- Attach any evidence to the form.
- Use additional sheets of paper if you need to.

Late appeal and application for extension of time

AIT-1(5.05) Rule 6, Asylum and Immigration Tribunal (Procedure) Rules 2005. Version 1.2 [12 May 2005]   1 of 9

Section 3 — Personal information

A Your Surname or family name
Please use CAPITAL LETTERS

B Your other names

C Address where you can be contacted
Notice:
If you change your address, you **must** notify the Asylum and Immigration Tribunal immediately, in writing. The address of the Tribunal is at the end of this form.

- Number/Street
- Town
- Post Code

D Telephone number
Give a number where the Tribunal may contact you during the day

E Your date of birth
Please give as Day/Month/Year

 / /

F Are you male or female?
Male ☐ Female ☐

G Nationality (or nationalities) or citizenship

H Do you have a representative?
No ☐ Yes ☐
Your representative should complete Section 6 on page 8.

I Have you appealed against any other immigration decision made in the United Kingdom?
No ☐ Yes ☐
What type of decision did you appeal against?
Asylum ☐ Non-asylum ☐
Date of the appeal / /
What is the appeal number, if you know it?

J 1 To the best of your knowledge, does any member of **your family** have an appeal pending in the United Kingdom?
No ☐ Yes ☐

Name(s)	Relationship	Appeal number, if you know it

AIT-1(5.05) Rule 6, Asylum and Immigration Tribunal (Procedure) Rules 2005. Version 1.2 [12 May 2005]

Supplement 1 — November, 2005

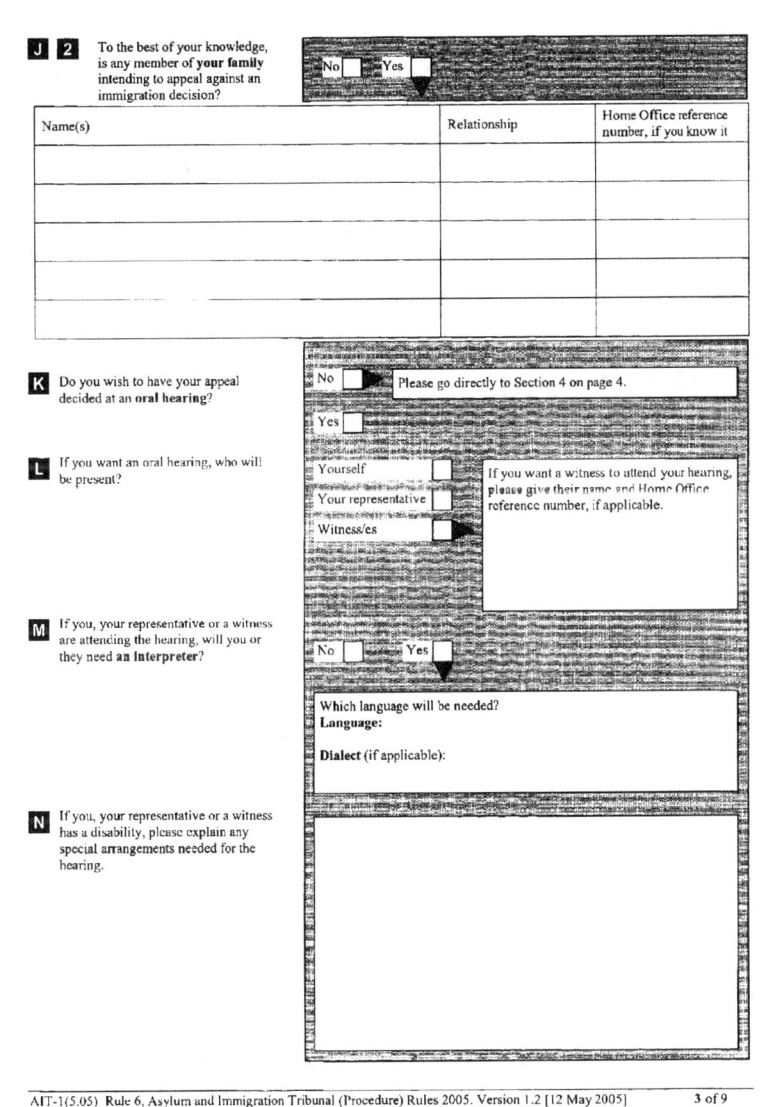

J 2 To the best of your knowledge, is any member of **your family** intending to appeal against an immigration decision?   No ☐   Yes ☐

Name(s)	Relationship	Home Office reference number, if you know it

K Do you wish to have your appeal decided at an **oral hearing**?

No ☐ — Please go directly to Section 4 on page 4.

Yes ☐

L If you want an oral hearing, who will be present?

Yourself ☐
Your representative ☐
Witness/es ☐

If you want a witness to attend your hearing, please give their name and Home Office reference number, if applicable.

M If you, your representative or a witness are attending the hearing, will you or they need **an interpreter**?   No ☐   Yes ☐

Which language will be needed?
Language:

Dialect (if applicable):

N If you, your representative or a witness has a disability, please explain any special arrangements needed for the hearing.

AIT-1(5.05) Rule 6, Asylum and Immigration Tribunal (Procedure) Rules 2005. Version 1.2 [12 May 2005]

Section 4 — Grounds of your appeal

In this section you must set out the **grounds for your appeal** and give **the reasons** in support of these grounds – that is, why you disagree with the decision. You must do this **now** because you may not be allowed to mention any further grounds at a later date.

- If your appeal relates in whole or in part to an **asylum** decision, complete all of boxes **A** to **E** that apply to you.
- If you are not sure which boxes apply to you or there are other points of the refusal letter that you disagree with, write your grounds in box **F**.
- If your appeal relates to a **non-asylum** decision, go to box **G** and complete it.

Please refer to the paragraphs of the refusal letter when possible.

You should include in this section any parts of your claim that you think have not been addressed in the refusal letter. You must say if you have raised these issues before.

Give as much detail as possible; use additional sheets of paper if you need to.

Asylum decision

A If you disagree with the Home Office's interpretation of **the situation in your country**, please explain why in this box, and give reasons to support your point of view.

B If the Home Office has suggested that you could **live safely in another part of your country of origin**, and you disagree, please explain why in this box.

AIT-1(5.05) Rule 6, Asylum and Immigration Tribunal (Procedure) Rules 2005. Version 1.2 [12 May 2005]

Supplement 1 — November, 2005

C If the Home Office has stated that your claim is **not credible**, and you disagree, please explain why in this box.

D If the Home Office has stated that you do not qualify as a refugee on grounds of race, religion, nationality, membership of a particular social group, or political opinion **(under the criteria of the 1951 Geneva Convention)**, and you disagree, please explain why in this box.

E If the Home Office has stated that specific articles of the **European Convention on Human Rights** (ECHR) do not apply to your case, and you disagree, please explain why in this box.

F If there is **anything else** that you disagree with in the Home Office letter, please explain why in this box.

☐ Please now go to section 5, 'Statement of additional grounds', on page 7.

Non-asylum decision

G If your appeal relates to a non-asylum decision with which you disagree, you must give your reasons below and refer to the paragraphs of the refusal letter.

SUPPLEMENT 1—NOVEMBER, 2005

Section 5

Statement of additional grounds

If your notice of decision requires you to make a **Statement of additional grounds**, you should make the statement in this box.
This section refers to any **other reasons** why you think:
- you should be allowed to stay in the United Kingdom, including any reasons relating to the European Convention on Human Rights
- you should not be removed or required to leave.

Do not repeat here any grounds and reasons that you have already given in Section 4.

You must give all these additional grounds and reasons **now** because you may not be able to make any other applications to appeal if this current application is refused. You should explain why you did not give these reasons before.

Section 6 — Representation

If you have a representative, he or she must complete this section.

A Declaration by the Representative

I, the representative, am giving this notice of appeal in accordance with the appellant's instructions, and the appellant believes that the facts stated in this notice of appeal are true.

Representative's signature and date

B Name of the representative
Please use CAPITAL LETTERS

C Name of the representative's organisation

D Postal address of organisation

Number / Street

Town

Post Code

E Reference for correspondence

F Telephone number

G Mobile number

H Fax number

I Email address

J Are you an organisation regulated by the Office of the Immigration Services Commissioner (OISC)?

☐ No ☐ Yes   Please provide the OISC reference:

K Has the appellant been granted publicly funded legal representation?

☐ No ☐ Yes   Please provide the LSC reference number, if applicable:

Notice to representatives

You must also notify the Asylum and Immigration Tribunal, and other parties, if you cease to represent the appellant. If the appellant changes representative, details of the new representative should be sent to the same address to which you are sending this form. Please give the **appellant's full name, address,** and **Home Office reference number.**

AIT-1(5.05) Rule 6, Asylum and Immigration Tribunal (Procedure) Rules 2005. Version 1.2 [12 May 2005]

SUPPLEMENT 1—NOVEMBER, 2005

Section 7

Declaration by appellant

If you are the appellant and you are completing this form yourself, you must complete the declaration.

A Declaration by the Appellant

I, the appellant, believe that the facts stated in this notice of appeal are true.

Appellant's signature and date

/ /

B Name of appellant
Please use CAPITAL LETTERS

Section 8

When you have completed the form

What to do next

Keep a copy of this form for your own use. Then **either**:
- send the original form to: **Asylum and Immigration Tribunal**
  PO Box 7866
  Loughborough
  LE11 2XZ
- or fax the form to: **01509 221699**

Send the notice of decision with this form.

To make sure that you are sending your notice of decision with this form, please tick this box. ☐

If you do not send the notice of decision with the appeal form, you must state the reason here.

Documents to support you application

If you are sending any other documents with this form to support your appeal, please list them here.

If you are intending to send other documents that are not yet available to you, please list them here.

If you need to contact the Tribunal

If you need to contact the Asylum and Immigration Tribunal, use your Home Office reference number and your Case Outcome ID in your correspondence.

Changes to your personal information

You must notify the Tribunal if you change your address, and/or if you appoint a new representative.

Data Protection Statement

Information, including personal details, that you have provided in this form will not be used by the Asylum and Immigration Tribunal for any purpose other than the determination of your application. The information may be disclosed to other government departments and public authorities only, for related immigration or asylum purposes.

Section 4: Grounds of appeal

NB: Previous practice was often to plead formulaic and unparticularised Grounds of Appeal, with the matter left to argument at the hearing before the adjudicator. The format of the new Form AIT-1 requires the Grounds to be more detailed.

Introduction

1. The Appellant ("A") is a citizen of Eastland and of Romany origin. He arrived in the United Kingdom clandestinely on [date] in a lorry and was apprehended by the immigration authorities. He immediately claimed asylum. He was interviewed by the immigration officials on [date]. The Secretary of State ("SSHD") considered his claim for asylum substantively but refused it on [date].

Factual basis for the claim for asylum

2. The basis for A's claim for asylum is explained in his asylum interview and in the witness statement dated [date], which the Tribunal should consider pursuant to s.85(4) of the Nationality, Immigration and Asylum Act 2002. In summary, A's case is that he has suffered persecution at the hands of nationalist and skinhead groups in Eastland, and that the authorities of that country have been unwilling or unable to offer him sufficient protection.

3. In particular:
   (a) Throughout his school life, he was bullied by other pupils whose families supported nationalist parties. He was twice injured so badly that he had to be taken to hospital. He complained to the school authorities but they did nothing. Similar treatment was experienced by his siblings who attended the same school.
   (b) After leaving school, he sought to find employment. This search took a long time as potential employers discriminated against him by reason of his ethnicity. He was often without money, and had to resort to sleeping rough, where he was frequently beaten up by local groups of skinheads. He complained to local police, but they refused to take his details and said that they would not help "dirty gypsies" like him.
   (c) In an attempt to improve his situation, in [date] he moved to a different town in another part of Eastland, where after some further time he succeeded in finding menial employment. However, in [date] the nationalist party ("NPE") gained several seats in a local election and became increasingly vocal in their calls to rid the country of non-Eastlanders, in particular those of Romany origin. The NPE would organise marches in the town, and its supporters would assault individuals whom they perceived to be of non-Eastland (and in particular Romany) origin.
   (d) In [date], the house in which A lived was daubed with graffiti saying "Gypsies get out". In [date] the house was burned down by persons whom A inferred were associated with the NPE. On the same night, two other houses in which Romanies lived were the subject of arson attacks.
   (e) In [date] two Romany men in the town were murdered and the NPE issued a statement saying that the men had only themselves to blame given that they were "parasites".
   (f) After a NPE march in [date], a group of NPE supporters came across A on his way home from work and seriously assaulted him, leaving him uncon-

scious with a broken right leg and left arm, multiple facial scars and internal haemorrhaging. During the course of the assault, the attackers told him to get out of Eastland or he would be killed.
(g) A was taken to hospital and when sufficiently recovered, made a complaint to the police in [date]. He gave them a detailed description of his attackers, and the name of one of them (whom he had recognised as a local leader of the NPE). However, the police did nothing to follow up his report. A learned that the NPE were paying regular bribes to the police (whose wages are very low) to purchase their inaction.
(h) In [date], A decided that he had no choice but to flee Eastland. He arrived in the UK after having passed through several other countries.

Reasons for SSHD's refusal

4. In his refusal letter of [date] the SSHD:
(a) Doubted A's credibility, stating that someone genuinely in fear of persecution would have claimed asylum in the first available country rather than waiting until arrival in the UK, relying on s.8(4) of the Asylum and Immigration (Treatment of Claimants, etc) Act 2004 ("the 2004 Act").
(b) Stated that A could have availed himself of the protection of the authorities of Eastland, and
(c) Stated that A could have availed himself of the internal flight alternative by going elsewhere in Eastland to escape the persecution.

Grounds of appeal

Section 4A: Country situation

5. The SSHD erred in finding that A could have availed himself of the protection of the Eastland authorities:
(a) The legal position was considered by the Court of Appeal in *R. (Bagdanavicius) v SSHD* [2004] 1 W.L.R. 1207. At [55], Auld L.J. set out the following principles (at para.55):
  (i) In the context of the Refugee Convention, sufficiency of state protection, whether from state agents or non-state actors, means a willingness and ability on the part of the receiving state to provide through its legal system a reasonable level of protection from ill-treatment of which the claimant for asylum has a well-founded fear.
  (ii) The effectiveness of the system provided is to be judged normally by its systemic ability to deter and/or to prevent the form of persecution of which there is a risk, not just punishment of it after the event.
  (iii) Notwithstanding systemic sufficiency of state protection in the receiving state, a claimant may still have a well-founded fear of persecution if he can show that its authorities know or ought to know of circumstances particular to his case giving rise to his fear, but are unlikely to provide the additional protection his particular circumstances reasonably require.
  (iv) Similar principles as above apply to a claim founded on Article 3.
(b) The principle at sub-paragraph 5(a)(i) was upheld by the House of Lords in *R. (Bagdanavicius) v SSHD* [2005] 2 W.L.R. 1359. Lord Brown found

that where the ill-treatment feared is from the hands of non-state agents, in addition to showing a real risk of serious harm from such agents, the claimant has to show that the receiving country would not provide a reasonable level of protection against such harm.

(c) The factual position is as follows:
   (i) A sought on several occasions as set out above to avail himself of the protection of the police, to no avail. They either did not take any details of the attacks, or when (once) they did, no attempt was made to question the identified suspect or his associates.
   (ii) The attacks on A were not just isolated, but formed part of a pattern of persecution by NPE supporters against Romanies, as evidenced in particular by the murder of two Romany men and the arson attacks referred to above.
   (iii) The 2005 US State Department Report (at para.3.10) and the Home Office Country Information and Policy Unit Report (at para.4.17), both of which are filed with this Form, note (a) the existence of frequent attacks on Romany people in various parts of the country; (b) that the police service in Eastland is ridden with endemic corruption; and (c) that they frequently discriminate against Romany people. The report of a recent visit by Amnesty International to Eastland (also filed with this report) notes increasing links between the police and the NPE, and the funding of the former by the latter. Two local newspapers (from the towns where A resided), copies of which are also provided, report that the chiefs of police in those towns are on the NPE's pay-role.

(d) In these circumstances it could not be said that there is a willingness and/or ability to provide through the legal system a reasonable level of protection against the NPE's actions. In any event, even if there is a systemic sufficiency of state protection in Eastland, A's past experience shows that the authorities know of circumstances particular to his case giving rise to his fear, but are unlikely to provide the additional protection his particular circumstances reasonably require.

Section 4B: Internal flight alternative

6. The SSHD erred in stating that A could have availed himself of the internal flight alternative. A had moved to a different part of Eastland to escape the persecution, to no avail. None of the objective country reports referred to above provide evidence of particular areas of Eastland where the threat from the NPE is lower than in the towns in which A resided. Alternatively, it would have been unduly harsh to expect A to move to any other part of Eastland, given that he would be unable to obtain any work, and would be unable to find any accommodation elsewhere in Eastland (Romanies being denied access to social housing in Eastland, and A having no relatives who could accommodate him).

Section 4C: Credibility

7. The SSHD erred in doubting A's credibility:
(a) A did not claim asylum in any other country on his way to the UK because he believed he would obtain a fairer determination of his case here and because he believed that the treatment of Romanies in the countries

through which he had travelled would be poor. The SSHD's doubt as to A's credibility on this basis alone was unreasonable. Insofar as this factor adversely affects A's credibility, very little weight should be attached to it.

(b) Further, the injuries suffered by A are now supported by a medical report dated [date] obtained from Dr A, a consultant accident and emergency physician at Binghampton General Hospital, whose report confirms the existence of the fractures A suffered in his attack (and that they were consistent with blows from blunt objects) and the existence of recent facial scarring. A copy of the report is filed with this form.

Section 4E: European Convention on Human Rights

8. Removal of A from the UK would be contrary to the SSHD's obligations under s.6 of the Human Rights Act 1998 because it would infringe his right under Article 3 of the European Convention on Human Rights ("ECHR"). Were A to be returned to Eastland, he would suffer inhuman and degrading treatment at the hands of the NEP from which he would gain no protection from the authorities, for the reasons given above.

Section 5: Statement of additional grounds

9. Furthermore, removal of A from the UK would infringe his right under Article 8 of the ECHR. A's parents are no longer alive and he has no contact with any relatives in Eastland. However, his two younger brothers (aged 16 and 17), who arrived in this country 6 months before A, have both been granted Indefinite Leave to Remain as refugees. A has lived with them since arrival in the UK, and they are a close family unit, depending on each other for emotional support. They look to him as a protector and mentor in the absence of any other relatives here. Removal to Eastland would (a) interfere with his family life with his brothers under Article 8(1); and (b) be disproportionate under Article 8(2). The circumstances of this case are so exceptional on its particular facts that the imperative of proportionality demands an outcome in A's favour: *Huang v SSHD* [2005] EWCA Civ 105 at [59].

57–04.1 *Insert Form AIT/103A (Application for Reconsideration), AIT:*

AIT/103A (Application for Reconsideration) (In Country Application)
s.103A Nationality, Immigration and Asylum Act 2002
(Civil Procedure Rule 54.29(1))

To: Asylum and Immigration Tribunal
PO Box 6987
Leicester   LE1 6ZX
Fax 0116 249 4214

APPLICATION NOTICE

I/We* apply for reconsideration of the decision of the Asylum and Immigration Tribunal on an appeal under s.82*/83* of the Nationality, Immigration and Asylum Act 2002.

Part A

Full Name of Applicant:
Address:
Date of birth:
Home Office Ref No:
AIT Ref No:
Date of Tribunal decision on appeal:
Was your case dealt with under the fast track procedure in the AIT? Yes/No*
Deemed Date of receipt of AIT decision**:
*(If your case was dealt with under the fast track procedure and you are seeking to file this application more than 2 days after the deemed date of receipt, or if your case was **not** dealt with under the fast track procedure and you are seeking to file this application more than 5 days after the deemed date of receipt, you must apply for an extension of time in which to file this application. In either case, your grounds for extension of time should be set out in Part B below)*
Filed by - (Applicant) (Litigation friend) (Applicant's Solicitor) (Charity or Not for Profit Organisation) (Signing on behalf of firm or company)'
Solicitor's reference No (if applicable):
Solicitor's Name (if applicable):
Address:***
Tel:
Fax:

* delete as appropriate
** If you were the Respondent to the appeal and were required to serve the notice from the Tribunal on the appellant, please state the date on which, and the means by which, the notice from the Tribunal was served.
*** If you are being assisted by a charity or not for profit organisation, you may give that organisation's address for the purpose of correspondence.

AIT/103A

Supplement 1 — November, 2005

Part B – Grounds for extension of time

(If you are seeking to file this application out of time (see explanation under Deemed Date of receipt of AIT decision in Part A), you must apply for an extension of time and set out in this Part the grounds on which it is contended that this application notice could not reasonably practicably have been filed within the appropriate time limit. Those grounds must be supported by written evidence verified by a statement of truth.)

Statement of Truth (to be signed when part B is completed)

(I believe*)(The Applicant believes*) that the facts contained under part B in this application notice are true.

I am duly authorised by the Applicant to sign this statement*

Full name_____

Name of Applicant's Solicitor's firm*_____

Signed_____ position or office held _____

(Applicant) (Litigation Friend) (Applicant's Solicitor) (Charity or Not for Profit Organisation) (Signing on behalf of firm or company)*

_____

*delete as appropriate

AIT/103A

Part C - Grounds upon which it is contended that the Tribunal made an error of law which may have affected its decision and reasons in support of those grounds:

SUPPLEMENT 1—NOVEMBER, 2005

Part D – Is an order for the payment of costs from the Community Legal Service Fund sought under s.103D of the Nationality, Immigration and Asylum Act 2002?

Yes/No/Not Applicable*

Note: *If an order for costs is sought you must answer "yes" to ensure that consideration is given to whether or not an order should be made.*

Unrepresented parties, if you do not have a legal representative acting for you, or you do not have a not charity or not for profit organisation assisting you, you must answer "Not Applicable"

If you were the Respondent to the original appeal, you must also answer "Not Applicable".

Signed **	(name)
(Applicant) (Litigation friend) (Applicant's Solicitor) (Charity or Not for Profit Organisation) (Signing on behalf of firm or company)*	
Address for Service:	
Dated:	

** If you are acting in person you must sign this form personally and give an address for service in England or Wales. If you are being assisted by a charity or not for profit organisation, you may give their address as your address for service.

You must file with this application notice-

(a) the notice of the immigration, asylum or nationality decision to which the appeal related;

(b) any other document which was served on you giving reasons for that decision;

(c) the grounds of appeal to the Tribunal;

(d) the Tribunal's determination on the appeal;

(e) any other documents material to the application which were before the Tribunal;

(f) written evidence in support of part B, where applicable.

*delete as appropriate

Please send your completed application, together with a copy, to The Asylum and Immigration Tribunal at the address shown on the front of this form.

ATT/103A

BULLEN & LEAKE & JACOB'S PRECEDENTS OF PLEADINGS

Insert Form PF244 R.C.J. (Application for Reconsideration), Administrative Court:

57–04.2

PF 244 R.C.J. (Application for Reconsideration) (In Country Application)
NOTICE under CPR 54.31(2)

Administrative Court Office ref CO/	/

s.103A Nationality, Immigration and Asylum Act 2002 and para 30(5)(b) of Schedule 2 to the Asylum and Immigration (Treatment of Claimants, etc.) Act 2004, (Civil Procedure Rule 54.31(2))

To: The Administrative Court Office
Room C315, Royal Courts of Justice, Strand, London WC2A 2LL

I/We* apply for an order that the Asylum and Immigration Tribunal reconsider its decision on an appeal under s.82*/83* of the Nationality, Immigration and Asylum Act 2002, following the Tribunal's decision not to order reconsideration

Part A

Full Name of Applicant:
Address:
Date of birth:
Home Office Ref No:
Reporting Centre (if applicable):
AIT Ref No:
Date of Tribunal decision on application for reconsideration:
Was your case dealt with under the fast track procedure in the AIT? Yes/No*
Deemed Date of receipt of AIT decision:** *(if your case was dealt with under the fast track procedure and you are seeking to file this application more than **2** days after the deemed date of receipt, or if your case was **not** dealt with under the fast track procedure and you are seeking to file this application more than **5** days after the deemed date of receipt, you must apply for an extension of time in which to file this application. In either case, your grounds for extension of time should be set out in Part B below)*
Filed by - (Applicant) (Litigation friend) (Applicant's Solicitor) (Charity or Not for Profit Organisation) (Signing on behalf of firm or company)*
Solicitor's reference No (if applicable):
Solicitor's Name (if applicable):
Address:***
Tel:
Fax:

*delete as appropriate
**If you were the Respondent to the appeal and were required to serve the notice from the Tribunal on the appellant, please state the date on which, and the means by which, the notice from the Tribunal was served.
***If you are being assisted by a charity or not for profit organisation, you may give that organisation's address for the purpose of correspondence.

PF244/103A/ACO

Part B – Grounds for extension of time

(If you are seeking to file this application out of time (see explanation under Deemed Date of receipt of AIT decision in Part A), you must apply for an extension of time and set out in this Part the grounds on which it is contended that the application notice could not reasonably practicably have been filed within the appropriate time limit. Those grounds must be supported by written evidence verified by a statement of truth.)

Statement of Truth (to be signed when part B is completed)

(I believe*)(The Applicant believes*) that the facts contained under part B in this application notice are true.

I am duly authorised by the Applicant to sign this statement*

Full name_____

Name of Applicant's Solicitor's firm*_____

Signed_____ position or office held _____

(Applicant) (Litigation Friend) (Applicant's Solicitor) (Charity or Not for Profit Organisation) (Signing on behalf of firm or company)*

*delete as appropriate

PF244/103A/ACO

Part B – Grounds for extension of time

(If you are seeking to file this application out of time (see explanation under Deemed Date of receipt of AIT decision in Part A), you must apply for an extension of time and set out in this Part the grounds on which it is contended that the application notice could not reasonably practicably have been filed within the appropriate time limit. Those grounds must be supported by written evidence verified by a statement of truth.)

Statement of Truth (to be signed when part B is completed)

(I believe*)(The Applicant believes*) that the facts contained under part B in this application notice are true.

I am duly authorised by the Applicant to sign this statement*

Full name_____

Name of Applicant's Solicitor's firm*_____

Signed_____ position or office held _____

(Applicant) (Litigation Friend) (Applicant's Solicitor) (Charity or Not for Profit Organisation) (Signing on behalf of firm or company)*

*delete as appropriate

PF244/103A/ACO

Part C — The grounds which the Court will consider are those you submitted to the AIT in your application for reconsideration (Form AIT/103A).

If you wish to respond to the reasons given by the Tribunal for it's decision that it does not propose to make an order for reconsideration, you should set out in this Part the grounds upon which you dispute any of the reasons given by the Tribunal and give reasons in support of those grounds.

PF244/103A/ACO

Part D – Is an order for the payment of costs from the Community Legal Service Fund sought under s.103D of the Nationality, Immigration and Asylum Act 2002?

Yes/No/Not Applicable*

Note: *If you are seeking an order for costs you must answer "yes" to ensure that consideration is given to whether or not an order should be made.*

Unrepresented parties, if you do not have a legal representative acting for you, or you do not have a charity or not for profit organisation assisting you, you must answer "Not Applicable".

If you were the Respondent to the original appeal, you must also answer "Not Applicable".

Signed **	(name)
(Applicant) (Litigation friend) (Applicant's Solicitor) (Charity or Not for Profit organisation) (Signing on behalf of firm or company)*	
Address for service:	
Dated:	

** If you are acting in person you must sign this form personally and give an address for service in England or Wales. If you are being assisted by a charity or not for profit organisation, you may give their address as your address for service.

You must file with this notice:

(a) A copy of the Tribunal's decision on your application for reconsideration;
(b) any other document which was served on you giving reasons for that decision;
(c) written evidence in support of part B, where applicable;
(d) A copy of your application for reconsideration (Form AIT/103A) as submitted to the AIT; and
(e) A cheque or postal orders for the issue fee of £400.00 or an Application for Fee Exemption or Remission in form EX160, if appropriate.

Note: Cheques or postal orders should be made out to Her Majesty's Courts Service.

* delete as appropriate

Please send your completed application, together with an additional copy, to The Administrative Court Office, Room C315, Royal Courts of Justice, Strand, London WC2A 2LL.

PF244/103A/ACO

SUPPLEMENT 1—NOVEMBER, 2005

Insert Form AIT-4 (Application to the Asylum and Immigration Tribunal for permission to appeal to the Court of Appeal or Court of Session):

57–04.3

ASYLUM AND IMMIGRATION (TREATMENT OF CLAIMANTS, ETC.) ACT 2004

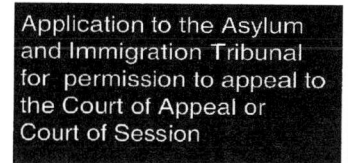

Application to the Asylum and Immigration Tribunal for permission to appeal to the Court of Appeal or Court of Session

Form AIT-4

Complete this form if you want to challenge the Asylum and Immigration Tribunal determination **on a point of law** by appealing to the Court of Appeal, or the Court of Session when the decision of the Tribunal was made in Scotland

- Please complete this form in English. It is in your interest to complete this form as thoroughly as possible, and state all your grounds in order for your application to be dealt with efficiently.
- Please complete Section 1 of this form by referring to the determination that the Tribunal sent you.
- Where there is a check box ☐, put a check (**X**) in it to show your answer.
- You should send your determination with this form.

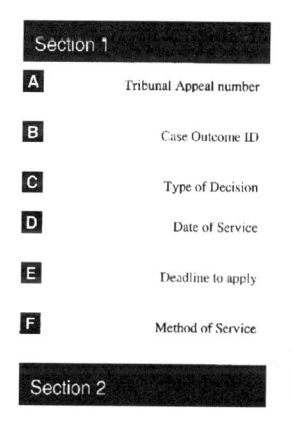

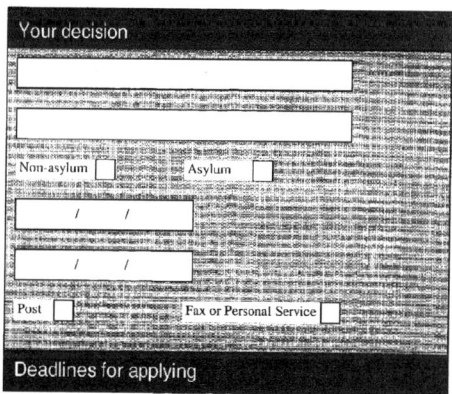

Section 1

- **A** Tribunal Appeal number
- **B** Case Outcome ID
- **C** Type of Decision
- **D** Date of Service
- **E** Deadline to apply
- **F** Method of Service

Your decision

Non-asylum ☐   Asylum ☐

/   /

/   /

Post ☐   Fax or Personal Service ☐

Section 2

Deadlines for applying

The deadline to apply is:

- **5 business days** from the date you were served with the decision, if you are detained under the Immigration Acts.
- **10 business days** from the date you were served with the decision, if you are not detained under the Immigration Acts.

Your application must be received by the Tribunal by the end of this period.

AIT-4 (4.05) Rule 34, Asylum and Immigration Tribunal Procedure Rules 2005

Section 3

Personal information

A Your Surname or family name
Please use CAPITAL LETTERS

B Your other names

C Address where you can be contacted
Notice:
If you change your address, you **must** notify the Asylum and Immigration Tribunal immediately, in writing. The address of the Tribunal is at the end of this form.

Number/Street

Town

Post Code

D Telephone number
Give a number where the Tribunal may contact you during the day

E Your date of birth
Please give as Day/Month/Year

/ /

F Are you male or female?

Male ☐ Female ☐

G Nationality (or nationalities) or citizenship

H Do you have a representative?

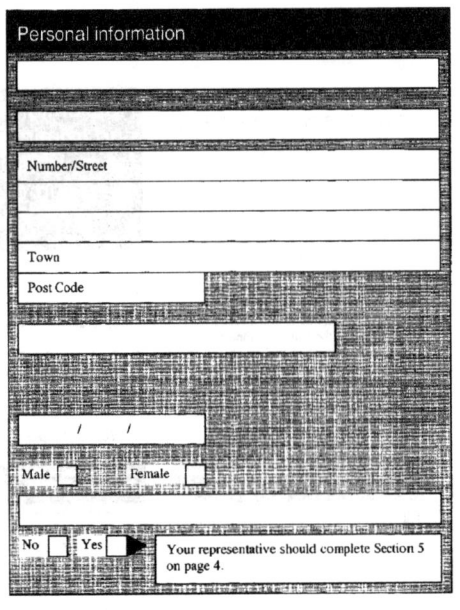

No ☐ Yes ☐ ▶ Your representative should complete Section 5 on page 4.

Please turn to section 4 on page 3 →

AIT-4 (4.05) Rule 34, Asylum and Immigration Tribunal Procedure Rules 2005

Supplement 1 — November, 2005

Section 4

Grounds of your appeal to the Court of Appeal or Court of Session

- An appeal to the Court of Appeal or Court of Session against a determination by the Tribunal is permissible only on a **point of law.**
- An appeal may be made against a point of law in a determination relating to an asylum decision or a non-asylum decision.
- In this section you must set out the **errors of law** that you believe have been made in the determination that you would like to appeal against and give **reasons** in support of these beliefs. You must do this **now** because you may not be allowed to mention any further points of law at a later date.
- Give as much detail as possible: use additional sheets of paper if you need to.

Section 5 — Representation

If you have a representative, he or she must complete this section.

A Declaration by the Representative

I, the representative, am making this application in accordance with the appellant's instructions, and the appellant believes that the facts stated in this application are true.

Representative's signature and date: _____ / _____ / _____

B Name of the representative
Please use CAPITAL LETTERS

C Name of the representative's organisation

D Postal address of organisation
- Number / Street
- Town
- Post Code

E Reference for correspondence

F Telephone number

G Mobile number

H Fax number

I Email address

J Are you an organisation regulated by the Office of the Immigration Services Commissioner (OISC)?
No ☐ Yes ☐ → Please provide the OISC reference:

K Has the appellant been granted publicly funded legal representation?
No ☐ Yes ☐ → Please provide the LSC reference number, if applicable:

Notice to representatives

You must notify the Asylum and Immigration Tribunal, and other parties, if you cease to represent the appellant. If the appellant changes representative, details of the new representative should be sent to the same address to which you are sending this form. Please give the **appellant's full name, address,** and **Tribunal appeal number.**

AIT-4 (4.05) Rule 34, Asylum and Immigration Tribunal Procedure Rules 2005

SUPPLEMENT 1 — NOVEMBER, 2005

Section 6

A Declaration by the Appellant

Appellant's signature and date

B Name of appellant
Please use CAPITAL LETTERS

Declaration by appellant

If you are the appellant and you are completing this form yourself, you must complete the declaration.

I, the appellant, believe that the facts stated in this application are true.

/ /

Section 7

What to do next

Send your determination with this form

Documents to support you application

If you need to contact the Tribunal

Changes to your personal information

Data Protection Statement

When you have completed the form

Keep a copy of this form for your own use. Then **either**:

❑ **send** the original form to:
    Asylum and Immigration Tribunal
    PO Box 6987
    Leicester
    LE1 6ZX

❑ or fax the form to: 0116 249 4214

To make sure that you are sending your determination with this form, please tick this box ☐

If you are sending any other documents with this form to support your application and appeal, please list them here.

If you need to contact the Asylum and Immigration Tribunal, use the Tribunal appeal number and your Case Outcome ID in your correspondence.

You must notify the Tribunal if you change your address, and/or if you appoint a new representative.

Information, including personal details, that you have provided in this form will not be used by the Asylum and Immigration Tribunal for any purpose other than the determination of your application. The information may be disclosed to other government departments and public authorities only, for related immigration or asylum purposes.

AIT-4 (4.05) Rule 34, Asylum and Immigration Tribunal Procedure Rules 2005

Replace precedent with:

57–05 Section 7 of Form N161: Grounds of Appeal

1. The AIT erred in law by setting aside the original Tribunal's finding on the question of financial support.

2. The AIT erred in law by finding the rule required sole responsibility to have been exercised continuously by the sponsor, up to and including the time of the application for entry clearance.

Section 8 of Form N161: Arguments in Support of the Appeal

References in square brackets are to the appeal bundle, and take the form [page number; paragraph number] where appropriate

Introduction

1. The Appellant ("A") is a national of Xland who sought entry clearance to join his mother ("M") in this country. He was born on September 1, 1995

2. A's application for entry clearance was made on October 3, 2004. The application was refused by the Respondent Entry Clearance Officer ("ECO") in Capital City, on November 25, 2004, after consideration of the documentary evidence submitted on A's behalf and after conducting separate interviews with A and M.

3. A appealed the ECO's refusal to the Asylum and Immigration Tribunal ("AIT"), pursuant to s.82(2) of the Nationality, Immigration and Asylum Act 2002 ("the 2002 Act"). The AIT ("the original Tribunal") allowed his appeal in a determination promulgated on April 5, 2005. The ECO made an application for reconsideration to the AIT under s.103A of the 2002 Act. This application succeeded and the matter was reconsidered by a differently constituted panel of the AIT ("the second Tribunal"), which allowed the appeal in a determination promulgated June 27, 2005.

4. A sought permission to appeal from the AIT to the Court of Appeal, which was refused on July 04, 2005.

The facts

5. The following facts were accepted by the original Tribunal.
   (a) M has lived in the UK since 1997. She was granted Indefinite Leave to Remain in 1998.
   (b) When she left Xland, she asked her brother and sister-in-law to look after A. However she made clear she would provide finance for all A's needs, and wished to be consulted on all important aspects of his upbringing.
   (c) M has spoken to A on the telephone at least once per week since her arrival, and has written letters to him every fortnight. She has given him advice and support on a range of questions, from friendships at school, to what books he might read.
   (d) She has been sent and has discussed with A all his school reports, and has discussed his extra-curricular activites with him such as his involvement in the local football team.
   (e) On arrival in this country M worked as an assistant nurse in a local private hospital. From then until shortly before the time of A's application for entry clearance, M sent regular money orders to her brother to cover all the expenses of raising A. However, when she was made redundant on July 1, 2004, she was no longer able to make those payments.

The law

6. A's application for entry clearance was made under para.297 of the Immigration Rules HC 395 (as amended). The full text of this rule is set out at [p.   ] and is not repeated here. The relevant sub-paragraph for the purposes of the present appeal is 297(i)(e).

7. The sole question for consideration by the AIT at both hearings was whether M had had "sole responsibility" for the A's upbringing within the meaning of para.297(i)(e).

8. In determining whether the sponsoring parent has had "sole responsibility" for the child under the Rules:

   (a) Every case will turn on its own facts.

   (b) The words cannot be construed literally. The fact that a relative or other carer in the foreign country where the applicant child has been living has taken some responsibility for the child's day to day life (*e.g.* making sure he is dressed, goes to school, eats properly, etc.) cannot by itself defeat the application: *Emmanuel v SSHD* [1972] Imm.A.R. 69.

   (c) To have sole responsibility, the relevant sponsor parent must have responsibility, albeit from a distance, for the direction or control of the important decisions in the child's life. *Ramos v IAT* [1989] Imm.A.R. 148; *Cenir v Entry Clearance Officer* [2003] EWCA Civ 572 at paras 7–8 *per* Buxton L.J.

   (d) A relevant factor will be to what extent the sponsor—as opposed to others—has financially supported the applicant: see, *e.g. Sloley v Entry Clearance Officer* [1973] Imm.A.R. 54.

   (e) Time on its own cannot be a conclusive factor: *Nmaju v Entry Clearance Officer* [2001] I.N.L.R. 26 at paras 19–25, *per* Schiemann L.J. A helpful question may be whether the sponsor has had sole responsibility for the child's upbringing for a "not insubstantial" period: see *R. v IAT Ex p. Uddin* [1986] Imm.A.R.203; *R. v IAT Ex p. Sajid Mahmood* [1988] Imm.A.R. 121; however this phrase is not to be regarded as if incorporated into the language of the rules.

9. A party may make an application for reconsideration on the grounds that the original Tribunal made an error of law: s.103A(1) of the 2002 Act. The appropriate court may order a reconsideration only if it thinks the original Tribunal may have made an error of law: s.103A(2) of the 2002 Act. Where a reconsideration pursuant to an order under s.103A is carried out, the second Tribunal must first decide whether the original Tribunal made a material error of law. If it decides that the original Tribunal did not make a material error of law, the second Tribunal must order that the original determination of the appeal shall stand: r.31(2), Asylum and Immigration Tribunal (Procedure) Rules 2005.

Ground 1

10. The second Tribunal found that M had not been in contact with A as she had claimed. The second Tribunal stated that had she done so, they would have expected to see corroborative evidence in the form of letters and telephone bills.

11. The second Tribunal erred as a matter of law in its approach. The original Tribunal had seen and heard M give evidence, had not doubted her credibility, and had expressly accepted that she had been in contact with A as described above. There was no error of law in the approach of the original Tribunal, nor had any been identified by the second Tribunal.

12. As such, it was impermissible for the second Tribunal to disturb the original Tribunal's findings of fact in this regard in the absence of a material error of law.

Ground 2

13. The second Tribunal erred in its approach in finding that because M had stopped making payments three months before the application (during which time A was financially supported by his uncle and aunt), M had not had sole responsibility for his upbringing:

(f) The second Tribunal misinterpreted para.297 as requiring continuous sole responsibility, including at the time of the application being made. It is clear from *Nmaju v Entry Clearance Officer* (above) that there is no requirement for continuous responsibility throughout the child's upbringing.

(g) In any event, the fact that financial payments had ceased for this period does not mean that M had ceased to have overall control and direction over the important decisions in A's upbringing.

Section 9 of Form N161

The order at s.5 be set aside. The Court of Appeal should declare that the sponsor has had sole responsibility for the Appellant's upbringing within the meaning of para.297 and that he should be granted entry clearance under that Rule.

Section 10 of Form N161

The Appellant does not with to make any other applications.

[Statement of Truth]

Replace precedent with:

57–06   **Section 8 of Form N461: Statement of Facts relied on**

1. By this judicial review application, the Claimant (C) challenges the decision of the Secretary of State for the Home Department (SSHD), by letter dated [date] and ongoing, refusing to accept that C's representations amount to a fresh asylum and human rights claim.

2. C, a Yland national, arrived in the UK by lorry on [date] and claimed asylum on the same day. At the asylum interview C claimed asylum on the basis of her membership of and campaigning activities for the National Opposition Party ("NOP"). C stated she was an active member of the NOP. She was detained and severely beaten by the Yland authorities on a number of occasions and as a result has visible scars on her body and face. She reported these incidents to the police but no action was taken.

3. Her claim was refused by the SSHD by letter dated [date].

4. C appealed this decision to the Asylum & Immigration Tribunal ("AIT"). The AIT dismissed C's appeal.

(a) The AIT accepted that C was an active member of the NOP and that she had been detained and severely beaten by the Yland authorities several years ago.

(b) The AIT concluded that while the objective country evidence documented numerous incidents of ill-treatment of NOP members occurring several years ago, there were no recent reports of similar incidents in respect of NOP members.

(c) The AIT accordingly held that there was no current real risk to C of prohibited ill-treatment.

5. C applied for reconsideration and the application was refused on [date].

6. Three months after the date of the AIT's determination, C obtained an expert report from Dr A at Holden University. Dr A, a distinguished academic on contemporary history and politics in Yland, concluded that:

(a) The ruling party in Yland is becoming increasingly totalitarian and paranoid about staying in power.

(b) This trend was exacerbated by a recent demonstration organised by the NOP. The demonstration was put down by the authorities using armed force. 50 NOP supporters were killed.

(c) The authorities in Yland are now regularly detaining and torturing NOP members.

(d) There are increasing reports of failed asylum-seekers to Yland being questioned by the Yland authorities. Where the returnees are suspected of NOP involvement, such interrogation frequently involves torture.

7. C made fresh representations to the SSHD, enclosing this report, and submitted that the representations amounted to a fresh claim for asylum under the Refugee Convention and Article 3 of the European Convention on Human Rights.

8. By letter dated [date], the SSHD refused to accept that the representations amounted to a fresh claim for asylum on the basis that C's claim, taking into account the report, did not have a realistic prospect of success. The SSHD reasoned that:

(a) The fresh claim was in substance no different from that originally advanced and rejected by the AIT.

(b) Many of the sources relied on by Dr A were oral; there was a lack of written, published and verifiable sources evidencing Dr A's conclusions.

(c) Even if Dr A's conclusions were accepted, there was no reason to think that on C's arrival in Yland airport the Yland authorities would suspect that she had previously been involved with the NOP.

Section 5 of Form N461: Detailed Statement of Grounds

9. Rule 353 of the Immigration Rules HC395 (the text of which is attached), provides that fresh representations will amount to a fresh asylum claim if they are significantly different from the material that has previously been considered; the submissions will only be significantly different if the content: (a) had not already been considered; and (b) taken together with the previously considered material, created a realistic prospect of success, notwithstanding its rejection.

10. A later claim may be a fresh claim if it is supported by fresh evidence of the same persecution said to be feared as was alleged in support of the earlier claim: *R. v Secretary of State for the Home Department Ex p. Boybeyi* [1997] Imm.A.R. 491.

11. As regards the phrase "realistic prospect", Nourse L.J. said that "it is not a very high test": *Boybeyi* (above) at 497.

12. The test outlined above is equally applicable to fresh human rights claims: *R. (Ratnam) v SSHD* [2003] EWHC 398 (Admin), para.12.

Grounds of challenge

13. The SSHD's refusal to accept C's representations as amounting to a fresh asylum and human rights claim was *Wednesbury* unreasonable and failed to take account of relevant factors.

14. Dr A is a leading academic and acknowledged expert on contemporaneous Yland history, society and politics. He has made numerous field trips to Yland and through his work is in touch with academics, politicians, journalists and civil servants (see his full CV, a copy of which is attached).

15. It is accepted that Dr A's conclusions in respect of the interrogation of failed asylum-seekers rely to a large extent on oral accounts rather than published material. However, this is not a reason for rejecting Dr A's conclusions as the Yland authorities are notorious for press and media censorship, as the objective country evidence demonstrates. Dr A's sources, as he explains in his report, are reliable and reputable.

16. The SSHD failed to appreciate that the evidence on the key point on which the first asylum claim was refused by the AIT (namely lack of risk to NOP members) had now fundamentally changed.

17. As a failed asylum who, as the AIT accepted, was previously an active member of the NOP with visible scars on her face and body as a result of past beatings, there is a real risk that C would attract the adverse attention of the Yland authorities on return.

18. For these reasons, the SSHD's decision to refuse to accept C's representations as amounting a fresh asylum claim was unlawful.

Section 6 of Form N461: Details of remedy

The Claimant seeks an order quashing the decision under challenge.

Part P

INSURANCE

Section 58: General Introduction

Utmost good faith

Add at end:

58–06 See *Drake Insurance Plc v Provident Insurance Plc* [2004] Q.B. 601, in which Pill L.J. suggested that the insurer's duty of good faith required it, before taking the draconian step of avoiding, to tell the insured what it had in mind and offer the insured the opportunity to comment on the proposed grounds of avoidance.

Add at end:

58–06.2 See *Drake Insurance Plc v Provident Insurance Plc* [2004] Q.B. 601 in which the Court of Appeal held insurers of a motor policy who operated a points system when deciding whether and on what terms to offer cover were not induced by the non-disclosure of a speeding conviction because if a full presentation had been made the insured would still have fallen within the same band of points.

Add at end:

58–06.3 See *Wise (Underwriting Agency) Ltd v Grupo Nacional Provincial* [2004] EWCA Civ 962 for a recent discussion of the circumstances in which an insurer will be held to have waived disclosure in the course of placement.

Post contract obligations of good faith

Add at end:

58–09 See also *Axa General Insurance Ltd v Gottlieb* [2005] EWCA Civ 112; [2005] 1 C.L.C. 62 in which the Court of Appeal held that the common law rule against the making of fraudulent claims resulted in the forfeiting of the entirety of any claim which was advanced by the insured fraudulently, including any interim payment made prior to the fraud and any sum that would have been payable if the claim had been advanced honestly.

Conditions precedent to liability

Notification of loss or circumstances.

Add at end:

58–10 The decision in *Alfred McAlpine v BAI (Run-Off) Ltd* has now in effect been overruled by the Court of Appeal's decision in *Friends Provident Life & Pensions Ltd v Sirius International Insurance* [2005] EWCA Civ 601, in which the court held that the normal rules as to repudiation applied to contract of insurance, with the result that the breach of an innominate term might, if sufficiently fundamental, entitle the insurer to repudiate the entire contract but would not entitle the insurer simply to reject a particular claim (as had been held to be the case in *McAlpine*).

Damages for late payment

Add at end:

58–13 See *Mandrake Holdings Ltd v Countrywide Assured Group Plc* [2005] All E.R. (D) 432, in which the Court of Appeal refused to allow an amendment to claim damages for late payment under a property insurance but indicated that the question of the recoverability of such damages was a controversial area of law which could and should be reviewed by the House of Lords.

Third Party rights

Add at end:

58–14 See *Re OT Computers Ltd (In Administration)* [2004] Ch. 317 in which the Court of Appeal held that: (a) the statutory transfer applied to all forms of liability insurance and not just to insurance in respect of liability in tort or contract for negligence (overruling the first instance decisions *Tarbuck v Avon Insurance Plc* [2002] Q.B. 571 and *T&N Ltd v Royal & Sun Alliance Plc* [2003] 2 All E.R. (Comm) 939; and (b) the transfer took place at the date of the relevant "insolvency event" (overruling the first instance decision of *Nigel Upchurch & Associates v The Aldridge Investment Co. Ltd* [1993] 1 Lloyd's Rep 535).

Pleading in insurance actions

Add at end:

58–15 In liability insurance if the insured reaches a settlement with the third party encompassing claims and counterclaims it will be necessary to ascertain the insured's legal liability to pay a sum to the third party and therefore to plead that liability following the decision of Colman J. in *Lumbermen Mutual Casualty Co. v Bovis Lend Lease Ltd* [2005] Lloyd's Rep. I.R. 74. A global settlement, without allocation, may therefore cause difficulties when seeking to recover against liability insurers.

Section 59: Motor Insurance

The provisions of the Road Traffic Act 1988
Add to second line of second paragraph, after "... to the assured":

or his authorised agent **59–02**

Add at end:

See also *Keeley v Pashen* [2004] EWCA Civ 1491 at [18].

The implementation of Fourth EC Motor Insurance Directive
Add at end of third paragraph:

(in conformity with what was then the draft Fifth EC Motor Insurance Directive, which has since been approved by the European Parliament in January 2005). **59–03**

Replace last sentence with:

See also Merkin and Stuart Smith, *The Law of Motor Insurance* (2004), para.5–195.

The obligations of the MIB
In the sixth paragraph, delete the text from the citation for Evans v Secretary of State for Environment to the end of the paragraph and replace with:

Case C–63/01, [2004] 1 C.M.L.R. 47. On the whole, the ECJ approved of the United Kingdom's implementation of the Second Directive, crucially ruling that the UK system by which the Second Directive is implemented through contractual agreements with a non-statutory body (the MIB) is a valid implementation of the Second Directive. Further, the ECJ largely endorsed the appeals system under the untraced drivers agreements which permits recourse on appeal to an arbitrator. The main impact of the decision is likely to be through the determinations that to satisfy the Second Directive the MIB must make provision in its awards in untraced driver cases for interest (or an analogous compensation for the effluxion of time), and that it may have to reimburse costs. The 2003 agreement has dealt with these issues, but the United Kingdom appears to have been in breach of European law before that. **59–04**

Add at end of seventh paragraph:

The operation of the exclusion was further considered in *Pickett v Roberts* [2004] EWCA Civ 6; [2004] 2 All E.R. 685.

Claim against third party's insurers by victim
At the beginning of paragraph 4, delete the words "The Claimant believes that". **59–P2**

SECTION 60: MISCELLANEOUS NON-MARINE INSURANCE

Add at end:

For a discussion of the problems which may arise in relation to the notification of **60–01** excess layer liability insurers see *Friends Provident Life & Pensions Ltd v Sirius International Insurance* [2005] Lloyd's Rep. I.R. 135 (Moore-Bick J.) and [2005] EWCA Civ 601.

Section 62: Life Insurance

In eighth line of third paragraph, after "Court of Appeal decision in Feasey", add: **62–01**

—a decision currently on appeal to the House of Lords

Reply alleging waiver, affirmation and estoppel following knowledge by the insurer of the disease

Add "]" to end of fourth line of paragraph 4. **62–P6**

Part Q

INTELLECTUAL PROPERTY

SECTION 64: PATENTS

Infringement.

Add at end:

For a general discussion of the law of patent infringement, see *Kirin-Amgen Inc v Hoechst Marion Rousell Ltd* [2005] R.P.C. 9. **64–02**

Add after para.64–12:

Streamlined procedure.

In cases where the trial is likely to last no longer than a day and there is limited or no cross examination and limited disclosure, it is possible to apply for the streamlined procedure as set out in the Patents Court Guide. The criteria are contained in para.10(b) of the Guide. It should be noted that legal advisors are under an obligation to draw their clients' attention to the availability of this procedure. In addition, the court may impose this procedure of its own volition. For a general discussion of this procedure, see *Research in Motion UK Ltd v (1) Impro Licensing Sarl (2) Lextron Systems, Inc* [2004] EWHC 1292 (Pat). **64–12.1**

Section 65: Confidential Information

Right of action.

Add at end:

The test under 3., above, might now better be viewed as whether the information has come to the recipient in circumstances where he has notice, or is held to have agreed, that the information is confidential. This may apply outside of a specific confidential relationship, for example, where the recipient finds an obviously confidential document which had inadvertently been dropped in the street. See *Campbell v MGN Ltd* [2004] 2 A.C. 457.

65–01

The Information.

Add at end:

In the context of private information pertaining to an individual, the test is one of whether the reasonable person would think there to be a "reasonable expectation" that the information would be kept private. See *Campbell v MGN Ltd* [2004] 2 A.C. 457 and *Michael Douglas v Hello! Ltd* [2005] EWCA Civ 595.

65–02

Personal relationships.

Add at end:

The law of breach of confidence in relation to personal relationships has been authoritatively reviewed and clarified in the cases of *Campbell v MGN Ltd* [2004] 2 A.C. 457 and *Michael Douglas v Hello! Ltd* [2005] EWCA Civ 595, to which the reader is referred.

65–08

Third Party Recipients.

Add at end:

After the decisions in *Campbell v MGN Ltd* [2004] 2 A.C. 457 and *Michael Douglas v Hello! Ltd* [2005] EWCA Civ 595 it may be queried whether the obligations upon third party recipients of confidential information may now be more onerous, applying where a reasonable person in the third party's position would have realised that the original owner of the information had a reasonable expectation that the information would be kept confidential.

65–09

Other influences.

Add at end:

At least in the cases of private information about individuals, the courts should apply the principles of, and European Court of Human Rights case law under, Arts 8 and 10 of the European Convention of Human Rights. See *Campbell v MGN Ltd* [2004] 2 A.C. 457 and *Michael Douglas v Hello! Ltd* [2005] EWCA Civ 595.

65–11

Section 66: Copyright, Related Rights and the Database Right

Copyright

Types of copyright work.

Add at end:

66–03 For the work needed to create a new copyright by correcting or updating an existing work, see *Sawkins v Hyperion Records Ltd* [2004] EWHC 1530; [2005] R.P.C. 4, Ch.

For the interaction between copyright works and design documents see para.67–02, below and *Lambretta Clothing Co. Ltd v Teddy Smith (UK) Ltd* [2004] EWCA Civ 886; [2005] R.P.C. 6.

The Database Right

Qualification and ownership.

Add at end:

66–21 For the decision of the ECJ, differing from the decisions of the English courts on the type of investment necessary for database rights to subsist, see [2005] R.P.C. 13.

Infringement.

Add at end:

66–22 For the decision of the ECJ see [2005] R.P.C. 13.

Defences

The Database Right

Grounds of defence.

Add at end:

66–28 For a general discussion of the database right, see the decision of the ECJ in *British Horseracing Board Ltd v William Hill Organisation Ltd* [2005] R.P.C. 13.

Section 67: Designs

Rights of action

"Ordinary copyright" under the 1988 Act.

Add at end:

For the interaction between copyright works and design documents see *Lambretta Clothing Co. Ltd v. Teddy Smith (UK) Ltd* [2004] EWCA Civ 886; [2005] R.P.C. 6. **67–02**

(National) design right.

Add at end:

For a discussion on using design rights in a "part of an article" to tailor the claim to catch the alleged infringement, see *Fulton (A.) Co. Ltd v Totes Isotoner (UK) Ltd* [2003] EWCA Civ 1514; [2004] R.P.C. 16. **67–03**

Section 68: Registered trade marks

Rights of Action.

Add at end of sub-paragraph (1):

In assessing identity of the sign and the trade mark, insignificant differences that may go unnoticed by an average consumer can be ignored. See Case C–291/00 *SA Societe LTJ Diffusion v Sadas Vertbaudet ("Arthur" and "Arthur et Felicie")* [2003] F.S.R. 34, ECJ at [50] to [54] and *Reed Executive Plc v Reed Business Information Ltd* [2004] R.P.C. 40.

68–01.1

At at end of sub-paragraph (2):

For a discussion of the scope of s.10(3) see the Opinion of the Advocate General in *Adidas-Salomon AG v Fitnessworld* [2004] F.S.R. 21 at [AG36] to [AG39].

Grounds of Defence

Defences by way of an application for invalidity.

Add at end of sub-paragraph (1):

; *Shield Mark BV v Kist (t/a Memex)* [2004] R.P.C. 17 (example of a sound sign) and *Libertel Groep BV v Benelux-Merkenbureau* [2004] F.S.R. 4 (example of a colour sign)

68–10

Add at end of first paragraph of sub-paragraph (3):

and *OHIM v WM Wrigley Jr Company (Doublemint)* [2004] R.P.C. 18

Add at end of sub-paragraph (4):

However, the shape of goods can be a trade mark where the shape is accepted by the public as such. Mere use might not be enough, what must be shown is that following such use the average consumer has come to rely upon the shape as denoting trade origin (*Bongrain SA's Trade Mark Application* [2005] R.P.C. 14).

Add after sub-paragraph (6):

(6a) That the application for the trade mark was made in bad faith. Bad faith is not limited to those instances involving actual dishonesty, but includes dealings which fall short of the standards of acceptable commercial behaviour observed by reasonable and experienced persons in the area under consideration. For a discussion of what constitutes bad faith see *Harrison's Trade Mark Application* [2005] F.S.R 10 at [20] to [34].

Defences by way of an application for revocation.

Add at end of first paragraph of sub-paragraph (1):

; *Ansul BV v Anjax Brandbereiliging BV* [2003] R.P.C. 40; *La Mer Technology Inc v Laboratiores Geomar SA* [2004] F.S.R. 38 and *Imaginarium Trade Mark* [2004] R.P.C. 30.

68–11

SECTION 69: PASSING OFF

For "Kerly's Law of Trade Marks and Trade Names (13th ed., 2001, Sweet & Maxwell)" substitute:

Kerly's *Law of Trade Marks and Trade Names* (14th ed., 2005, Sweet & Maxwell)

Goodwill.

Add at end of second paragraph:

Where the goodwill is shared it is possible for one co-owner to bring an action against the other (*Sir Robert McAlpine Ltd v Alfred McAlpine* [2004] R.P.C. 36). **69–02**

Add at end of third paragraph:

and *Radio Taxicabs (London) Ltd v Owner Drivers Radio Taxi Services Ltd* [2004] R.P.C. 19

Pleading

Relief claimed.

Add at end:

Damages are not confined to directly provable losses of sales. In particular, damages from wrongful association can be wider and cover damage to the exclusivity of the claimant's goodwill (*Sir Robert McAlpine Ltd v Alfred McAlpine* [2004] R.P.C. 36). **69–07**

Grounds of defence

Use of own name.

Add at end:

and *Reed Executive Plc v Reed Business Information Ltd* [2004] R.P.C. 40 **69–10**

Part R

JUDICIAL REVIEW

SECTION 70: APPLICATIONS FOR JUDICIAL REVIEW

When to use Part 54

In the first paragraph, delete ": Pt 54.1(2)(b), (c), (d)". **70–02**
In sixth line of second paragraph, after "if he is seeking damages", add:

, restitution or the recovery of a sum due

Venue

In the first paragraph, for "Law Courts, Cathays Park, Cardiff CF10 3PG: Practice Direction paras 2.2, 3", substitute:

Administrative Court in Wales, Civil Justice Centre, 2 Park Street, Cardiff, CF10 1ET: **70–04** Practice Direction paras 2.3, 3

Part S

PERSONAL INJURY

Section 71: Personal Injury

Heads of Liability in Particular Cases

Occupational/Employer's Liability

Add at end:

71–07 Per *William Majrowski v Guy's & St Thomas's NHS Trust* [2005] EWCA Civ 251, an employee can be vicariously liable under s.1 of the Protection From Harassment Act 1997 for their employees' breach of s.3 of the Act. Further, the existence of the duty and its breach in stress claims continues to be a very difficult area for claimants to establish. These practical difficulties have led to a more detailed Statement of Case and a third precedent in 71–S17A, below.[1]

It can be used for bullying claims and should also be referred to by those using 71–S16 and 71–S17 as it contains the Working Time Regulations 1998, the Health and Safety (Consultation with Employees) Regulations 1996 and enhancements to the statement of case under the Management of Health and Safety At Work Regulations 1992 and 1999.

Note 1: Grateful acknowledgment to Andrew Buchan for this statement of case.

Add at end:

71–07.1 The scope of the update is restricted as *per* note 4 to para.71–01, above to the most commonly breached statutory duties at work. Two significant statutory instruments are dealt with in this update, namely the Work at Height Regulations 2005 (SI 2005/735) and the Control of Vibration At Work Regulations 2005 (SI 2005/1093). The following further statutory instruments have come into force since publication of the 15th ed. and may need to be referred to depending on the circumstances and location of the original accident: the Manufacture and Storage of Explosives Regulations 2005 (SI 2005/1082); the Equipment and Protective Systems Intended for Use in Potentially Explosive Atmospheres (Amendment) Regulations 2005 (SI 2005/830); the Control of Substances Hazardous to Health (Amendment) Regulations 2004 (SI 2004/3386); the Manufacture and Storage of Explosives Regulations 2005 (SI 2005/1082); the Offshore Installations (Safety Zones) (No.3) Order 2004 (SI 2004/1746); the Offshore Installations (Safety Zones) Order 2004 (SI 2004/343); the Carriage of Dangerous Goods and Use of Transportable Pressure Equipment Regulations 2004 (SI 2004/568); the Dangerous Substances and Explosive Atmospheres Regulations 2002 (SI 2002/2776); the Loading and Unloading of Fishing Vessels Regulations 1988 (SI 1988/1656); the Quarries Regulations 1999 (SI 1999/2024); the Fire Precautions (Workplace) Regulations 1997 (SI 1997/1840); the Work in Compressed Air Regulations 1996 (SI 1996/1656).

Beginning a Claim: Protocols

Add after first sentence:

71–09 In appropriate claims reference should be made to the *Disease and Illness Claims Protocol*.

Employer's Liability

Add after 71–S11:

Claim under the Work At Height Regulations 2005[1]   71–S11A

1. [Set out the employment relationship between the parties AND/OR the fact that the Claimant was carrying out work under the Defendants control].

2. The Claimant was carrying out work at Height [set out the facts giving rise to the accident].

3. The Claimant believes that his accident was caused by the Defendants' breach of statutory duty and negligence in that they:

Particulars of Breach of Statutory Duty and Negligence

(1) In breach of reg.4 and or negligently failed to ensure that the work was:
   (a) properly planned;
   (b) appropriately supervised;
   (c) carried out in a manner was safe;
(2) Caused, allowed or permitted the Claimant to carry out the work when the weather conditions jeopardised his health or safety in breach of reg.4;
(3) Failed to ensure that the Claimant/Claimant's fellow workers were competent and or supervised by a competent person in respect of [set out the activity which should fall with any activity including organisation, planning and supervision in relation to work at height or work equipment for use in such work] in breach of reg.5;
(4) Failed to take account of a risk assessment under reg.3 of the Management Of Health Safety and Welfare Regulations 1999 in breach of reg.6;
(5) Failed to ensure that work was not carried out at height in breach of reg.6;
(6) In breach of reg.6 failed to ensure that suitable and sufficient measures were taken to prevent the Claimant falling a distance liable to cause personal injury including ensuring that the work was carried out including either ensuring the work was carried out from an existing place of work which complies with Sch.1 OR [if compliance with Sch.1 is not reasonably practicable] providing sufficient work equipment to prevent a fall occurring;
(7) Failed to provide sufficient work equipment to minimise the distance and consequences of a fall in breach of reg.6;
(8) Failed to provide such additional training and instruction or take other additional suitable and sufficient measures to prevent the Claimant falling a distance in breach of reg.6;
(9) In breach of reg.7 failed to give collective protection measures priority over personal protection measures and take account of:
   (a) the working conditions and the risks to the safety of persons at the place where the work equipment is to be used;
   (b) [in the case of work equipment for access and egress] the distance to be negotiated;
   (c) the distance and consequences of a potential fall;
   (d) the duration and frequency of use;
   (e) the need for easy and timely evacuation and rescue in an emergency;
   (f) any additional risk posed by the use, installation or removal of that work equipment or by evacuation and rescue from it [set out such risk];

(10) In breach of reg.7 failed to select work equipment which was appropriate to the nature of the work to be performed and or the foreseeable loadings and or allow passage without risk and or was most suitable;

(11) In breach of reg.8 failed to ensure that in the case of [delete as necessary]

a guard-rail, toe-board, barrier or similar collective means of protection (Sch.2) OR a working platform (Pt 1 of Sch.3) OR where scaffolding is provided (Pt 2 of Sch.3) OR a net, airbag or other collective safeguard for arresting falls which is not part of a personal fall protection system (Sch.4) OR a personal fall protection system (Pt 1 of Sch.5) OR in the case of a work positioning system (Pt 2 of Sch.5) OR in the case of rope access and positioning techniques (Pt 3 of Sch.5) OR in the case of a fall arrest system (Pt 4 of Sch.5) OR in the case of a work restraint system (Pt 5 of Sch.5) OR a ladder (Sch.6)[2] is complied with;

(12) Failed to ensure that no person passed across, near or works on, from or near, a fragile surface in breach of reg.9;

(13) Failed to ensure that suitable and sufficient platforms, coverings, guard rails or similar means of support or protection were provided and used and that loads were supported by such supports or borne by such protection in breach of reg.9;

(14) Failed to take suitable and sufficient measures to minimise the distances and consequences of the Claimants fall in breach of reg.9;

(15) Failed to display prominent warning notices at the approach to the place where the fragile surface was situated or make the Claimant aware of it by other means in breach of reg.9;

(16) Failed to take suitable and sufficient steps to prevent the fall of any material or object in breach of reg.10;

(17) Failed to take suitable and sufficient steps to prevent the Claimant being struck by any falling material or object in breach of reg.10;

(18) Failed to ensure that no material or object was thrown or tipped in breach of reg.10;

(19) Failed to ensure that materials and objects were stored in such a way as to prevent risk to any person arising from the collapse, overturning or unintended movement of such materials or objects in breach of reg.10;

(20) Failed to ensure that a danger area was equipped with devices preventing unauthorised persons from entering such area and that such an area was clearly indicated in breach of reg.11;

(21) Failed to inspect the work equipment in position in breach of reg.12[3];

(22) Failed to inspect the work equipment at suitable intervals and after an exceptional circumstance (set out the circumstance that was likely to jeopardise the safety of the work equipment) in breach of reg.12[4];

(23) Failed to ensure that the working platform was not used in any position unless it had been inspected in that position OR in the case of a mobile working platform, inspected on the site, within the previous 7 days in breach of reg.12[5];

(24) Failed to ensure that the surface and every parapet, permanent rail or other such fall protection measure of every place of work at height are checked on each occasion before the place is used in breach of reg.13;

Note 1: In force from April 6, 2005.

Note 2: It is beyond the scope of this update to set out the detail of each of the comprehensive schedules in full and reference should be made to the full statutory instrument.

Note 3: Regulation 12 applies to reg.8 and Schs 2 to 6.

Note 4: Regulation 12 applies to reg.8 and Schs 2 to 6.

Note 5: Regulation 12 applies to reg.8 and Schs 2 to 6.

Add after 71–S17:

71–S17A **Claim For Stress And Or Bullying At Work**

1. Repeat paras 1–9 of 71–S16 or paras 1–9 of 71–S17 and add factual details of bullying if appropriate.

Factors Informing Duty and Breach

2. Since 1995[1] the HSE has advised that stress should be treated like any other occupational health risk. An employer's Risk Assessment should include the risks of psychological as well as physical injury. Employers should carry out the risk assessment process by following the principles laid out in the HSE's publication 5 Steps to Risk Assessment.[2] The five steps are (1) Identify the hazards; (2) Decide who might be harmed and how; (3) Evaluate the risk by Identifying what action is already being taken and deciding whether it is enough and if it is not, deciding what more needs to be done; (4) Record the significant findings of the assessment; and (5) Review the assessment at appropriate intervals.

3. The guidelines for the management of occupational stress are generic. They are common to most jobs. Employers should have a health and safety policy. This ought to refer to the risk of occupational stress and the system that the employer has in place for reporting and managing it.

4. The latest relevant guidance on the management of occupational stress from the HSE is "Tackling Work-Related Stress."[3] This booklet, like the research and guidance published in 1993 by the HSE, highlights seven risk factors that contribute to the risk of injury from occupational stress. These are, Culture, Demands, Control, Relationships, Change, Role, Support, Training and Factors unique to the individual.

5. The Claimant believes that his injuries were caused by the negligence and breach of contract and the breach of statutory duty of the Defendants in that they:

Particulars of Breach of Statutory Duty and Negligence and Breach of Contract

(1) Caused the Claimant to be bullied and harassed whilst working with him. The Claimant will contend that the defendant is vicariously liable for the harassment of X, as set out above at para.10, pursuant to ss.1 and 3 of the Protection from Harassment Act 1997;

(2) Failed to consult the Claimant pursuant to reg.3 of the Health and Safety (Consultation with Employees) Regulations 1996 and or negligently failed to heed the provisions of the regulations in particular with regard to:

(a) the introduction of any measures at the workplace which may substantially affect the health and safety of the Claimant;

(b) arrangements for appointing or (as the case may be) nominating persons in accordance with regs 6(1) and 7(1)(b) of the Management of Health and Safety at Work Regulations 1992;
(c) any health and safety information the Defendant was required to provide to the Claimant by or under the relevant statutory provisions which included any matters affecting his health and safety;
(d) the planning and organisation of the health and safety training the Defendant was required to provide to the Claimant by or under any relevant statutory provisions;
(e) the health and safety consequences of new technology;

(3) Failed to assess the risk of the work required to be performed by the Claimant as required by reg.3 of the Management of Health and Safety at Work Regulations 1992 and 1999 or under its duty as employers and the Approved Code of Practice (ACOP), paras 9, 10, 16, 23, 24, 25, 26 and 27.
  (a) The Defendant was under this duty from 1st January 1993. It should have been clear to a competent person (reg.6) responsible for carrying out the suitable and sufficient risk assessment (following the guidelines set out in paras 12–27 of the ACOP) that after May 1995 and the publication of the Health and Safety Executive Guidelines on "Stress at work, Guidelines for Employers" there was a risk of psychological injury to the Claimant that needed to be assessed.
  (b) The results should have been recorded in writing (ACOP, paras 23–27). Had the Defendant properly assessed the Claimant's work, and reviewed (ACOP, para.10) that assessment when their was any material change to the Claimant's employment, it would have realised in good time that there was a potential risk of psychological injury.
  (c) The ACOP requires the Defendant to have regard to the general principles of risk assessment, to have regard amongst other things to HSE guidance (ACOP, para.9). Guidelines were published by the HSE on "How to tackle work related stress" in 1998. A resource pack for Management training and development entitled "Mental Well-being in the Workplace" was published in 1998 by the HSE.
  (d) Following the assessment the Defendant was under a duty to take the preventive and protective measures that had been identified (ACOP, para.27). It is the Claimant's case that any suitable and sufficient risk assessment would have identified the behaviour of the Defendant's servants or agents as giving rise to a risk of psychiatric injury. Preventive measures would or should have been taken and this would have avoided the Claimant's injuries;

(4) Failed to apply the principles of prevention set out in ACOP to the Management of Health and Safety at Work Regulations 1992 and Sch.1 and reg.4 of the 1999 Regulations);

(5) Failed to make and give effect to such arrangements as were appropriate for the effective planning, organisation, control, monitoring and review of measures to protect the Claimant pursuant to reg.4 of the Management of Health and Safety at Work Regulations 1992 (reg.5 of the 1999 Regulations) and the ACOP or under their duty as employers;

(6) Failed to provide the Claimant with such health surveillance as was appropriate pursuant to reg.5 of the Health and Safety at Work Regula-

tions 1992 (reg.6 of the 1999 Regulations) and the ACOP or under their duty as employers;

(7) Failed to establish and where necessary give effect to appropriate procedures to be followed in the event of the Claimant being exposed to a serious and imminent danger at work as required by reg.7 of the Management of Health and Safety at Work Regulations 1992 (reg.8 of the 1999 Regulations) and the ACOP or under their duty as employers;

(8) Failed to inform the Claimant of the risks to his health and safety identified by the assessments and the preventative and protective measures as required by reg.8 of the Management of Health and Safety at Work Regulations 1992 (reg.10 of the 1999 Regulations) and the ACOP or under their duty as employers;

(9) Failed to ensure that when entrusting tasks to the Claimant account was taken of his capabilities as regards health and safety, as required by reg.11(1) of the Management of Health and Safety at Work Regulations 1992 (reg.13 of the 1999 Regulations) and the ACOP or under their duty as employers;

(10) Failed to heed and/or act upon the Claimant's complaints pursuant to reg.12(2) of the Management of Health and Safety at Work Regulations 1992 (reg.14(2) of the 1999 Regulations);

(11) Failed to comply with the Working Time Regulations 1998 and or negligently failed to heed the regulations and their provisions;

(12) Failed to limit the Claimant's maximum weekly working time to 48 hours as required by reg.4;

(13) Failed to provide the Claimant with daily rest breaks as required by reg.10;

(14) Failed to provide the Claimant with regular breaks as required by reg.12;

(15) Failed to provide a weekly rest period as required by reg.11;

(16) Failed to supply the Claimant with annual leave as required by reg.13;

(17) Failed to organise the Claimant's pattern of work so that it was safe as required by reg.8;

(18) Failed to provide the Claimant with approved posters or leaflets published by the Health and Safety Executive pursuant to the Health and Safety Information for Employees Regulations 1989, reg.4 or under their duty as employers.

(19) Culture

Failed to have a positive culture in that:

(a) work-related stress and health issues were not treated seriously and the organisation did not respond positively to any concerns;

(b) there was not good, open, communication between employees and between employees and management;

(c) staff were not consulted and were not able to participate in decisions that may affect them;

(d) staff were not supported emotionally and practically;

(e) problems were not recognised nor solved promptly;

(f) working long hours were not discouraged;

(g) staff were not discouraged from taking work home.

(20) Demands

Placed excessive demands on their employees in that:
- (a) there were insufficient resources (in terms of ability, staff, time, or equipment) to cope with the work;
- (b) did not heed the fact that the Claimant was working excessive hours;
- (c) did not heed the fast pace at which the Claimant was required to work and the conflicting priorities which he had to resolve.

(21) Control
- (a) The Claimant was given little control in the distribution and amount of work;
- (b) The Claimant's complaints were ignored;
- (c) The Claimants role was changed without consultation.

(22) Relationships
- (a) The Claimant was bullied by X as set out at Paragraph 10 above and such bullying included [amend as appropriate] verbal abuse, insubordination, victimisation, humiliation or ridicule, libel, slander or malicious gossip, spying, pestering or other inappropriate intrusive questioning particularly into personal or domestic life, setting impossible or arbitrary objectives or deadlines, excessive supervision, unjustified fault finding, withholding information that the Claimant had a reasonable expectation of being given, exclusion from meetings that the employee has a reasonable expectation of attending or other forms of unreasonable ignoring of the employee, refusing without reasonable cause reasonable requests for leave or training, maliciously preventing career development; and
- (b) The bullying amounted to harassment.

(23) Change

Changing the Claimants status/reporting lines/job function/department/title without consultation;

(24) Role
- (a) The Claimant was put into role conflict by the demands of doing things which were not part of his job and or by reporting to two different managers;
- (b) The Claimant's role was ambiguous in that he did not have a clear picture of his work objectives or expectations of him or responsibilities of his job;
- (c) The Claimant's complaints were ignored.

(25) Support, training and factors unique to the individual
- (a) The Claimant was not given enough training to feel competent doing his job;
- (b) The Claimant was only ever reprimanded when his work was not to the required standard rather than supported;
- (c) The Claimant was not supported.

Note 1: "Stress at Work, a guide for employers", HSE 1995, HS(G)116, ISBN 0 717 60733 X.
Note 2: "5 Steps to risk assessment", INDG 163 (rev1) HSE Books, ISBN 0 717 61565 0.
Note 3: "Tackling work-related stress, a managers' guide to improving and maintaining employee health and well-being", HSE 2001, ISBN 0 717 62050 6.

Claim relating to Vibration White Finger AND/OR Vibration

Add after paragraph (28):

71–S21   The Control of Vibration at Work Regulations 2005[1]

(29) Exceeded the daily exposure limit for hand-arm vibration [or whole body vibration] and or failed to take action where the daily exposure action value was exceeded in breach of reg.4;

(30) In breach of reg.5 and/or negligently failed to carry out a suitable and sufficient assessment of the risk created by that work to the health and safety of those employees and particularly failed to assess the daily exposure to vibration by means of:

(a) observation of specific working practices;

(b) reference to relevant information on the probable magnitude of the vibration corresponding to the equipment used in the particular working conditions;

(c) measurement of the magnitude of vibration to which his employees are liable to be exposed;

(31) In breach of reg.5 and/or negligently the risk assessment did not include consideration of:

(a) the magnitude, type and duration of exposure, including any exposure to intermittent vibration or repeated shocks;

(b) the effects of exposure to vibration on employees whose health is at particular risk from such exposure;

(c) any effects of vibration on the workplace and work equipment, including the proper handling of controls, the reading of indicators, the stability of structures and the security of joints;

(d) any information provided by the manufacturers of work equipment;

(e) the availability of replacement equipment designed to reduce exposure to vibration;

(f) any extension of exposure at the workplace to whole-body vibration beyond normal working hours, including exposure in rest facilities supervised by the employer;

(g) specific working conditions such as low temperatures;

(h) appropriate information obtained from health surveillance including, where possible, published information;

(32) Failed to review the risk assessment shall regularly and, in any event where it was suspected the assessment was no longer valid and or there had been a significant change in the work to which the assessment related in breach of reg.5;

(33) Failed to ensure that risk from the exposure of his employees to vibration was eliminated at source in breach of reg.6;

(34) Failed to ensure that risk from the exposure of his employees to vibration was eliminated at source in breach of reg.6 was reduced to as low a level as was reasonably practicable;

(35) In breach of reg.6 failed to reduce exposure to as low a level as is reasonably practicable by establishing and implementing a programme of organisational and technical measures which is appropriate to the activity based on the principle of prevention and particularly:
   (a) using other working methods which eliminate or reduce exposure to vibration;
   (b) the choice of work equipment of appropriate ergonomic design which, taking account of the work to be done, produces the least possible vibration;
   (c) the provision of auxiliary equipment which reduces the risk of injuries caused by vibration;
   (d) appropriate maintenance programmes for work equipment, the workplace and workplace systems;
   (e) the design and layout of workplaces, work stations and rest facilities;
   (f) suitable and sufficient information and training for employees, such that work equipment may be used correctly and safely, in order to minimise their exposure to vibration;
   (g) limitation of the duration and magnitude of exposure to vibration;
   (h) appropriate work schedules with adequate rest periods;
   (i) the provision of clothing to protect employees from cold and damp;
(36) Failed to ensure that the Claimant was not exposed to vibration above the exposure limit value in breach of reg.6^2;
(37) In breach of reg.6^3 where the exposure limit was exceeded failed, forthwith to:
   (a) reduce exposure to vibration to below the limit value;
   (b) identify the reason for that limit being exceeded;
   (c) modify the measures taken in accordance with paragraphs (a) and (b) to prevent it being exceeded again;
(38) Failed to ensure that the Claimant was placed under suitable health surveillance in breach of reg.7;
(39) Failed to ensure that a suitably qualified person informed the Claimant of the identifiable disease [set it out] and or adverse health effect and ensure that:

[set out as appropriate]
   (a) information and advice was given to the Claimant in respect of further health surveillance;
   (b) the Defendants informed themselves of the significant findings [set them out] from this assessment of the Claimant;
   (c) a review of compliance measures in respect of reg.6 as set out above was undertaken;
   (d) consideration was given to the Claimant being assigned to alternative work where there is no risk from further exposure to vibration;
(40) In breach of reg.8 failed to provide the Claimant with suitable and sufficient information, instruction and training and or to update that information, instruction and training including:
   (a) the organisational and technical measures taken in order to comply with the requirements of reg.6;

(b) the exposure limit values and action values set out in reg.4;
(c) the significant findings of the risk assessment, including any measurements taken, with an explanation of those findings;
(d) why and how to detect and report signs of injury;
(e) entitlement to appropriate health surveillance under reg.7 and its purposes;
(f) safe working practices to minimise exposure to vibration;
(g) the collective results of any health surveillance undertaken in accordance with reg.7.

Note 1: In force from July 6, 2005, save in respect of paras (35) and (36) set out below.

Note 2: This part of reg.6 is not in force until not in force until July 6, 2010 (in forestry and agriculture not in force until July 6, 2014) for work equipment provided prior to July 6, 2007 but employer needs to take into account latest technical advances and organisational measures set out above under reg.6.

Note 3: This part of reg.6 is not in force until not in force until July 6, 2010 (in forestry and agriculture not in force until July 6, 2014) for work equipment provided prior to July 6, 2007 but employer needs to take into account latest technical advances and organisational measures set out above under reg.6.

Employer's Liability

Add new defence after 71–S35:

71–S35A   **Defence to Claim Under the Work At Height Regulations**

1. The Defendant believes that the Claimant caused or contributed towards his injuries in that, in breach of statutory duty he:

Particulars of Breach of Statutory Duty and Negligence

(1) Failed to report [insert activity] and or defect relating to the work which the Claimant knew was likely to endanger his or another's safety in breach of Regulation 14;
(2) Failed to use the work equipment/safety device provided to him in accordance with any training in the use of the work equipment or device concerned which have been received by him AND/OR the instructions respecting that use which have been provided to him in breach of Regulation 14;
(3) [Continue by taking the allegations in the Particulars and setting out a case, if possible, in respect of each of them]

Section 72: Clinical Negligence

Claims

Add after para.72–04:

72–04.1 The pleadings included in the clinical negligence section are, of necessity, variants on what would normally be expected in a personal injury action. There are a number of respects in which clinical negligence claims require different formulation. These are summarised below.
  (1) In clinical negligence cases it will inevitably be important to identify the appropriate defendant. The NHS is fragmented into a number of Health Authorities, however in the vast majority of cases the body responsible to meet a claim for clinical negligence, and therefore the appropriate defendant, will be an individual NHS Trust and/or a particular GP's practice. Identification of the correct defendant is of critical importance.
  (2) Where an individual health professional who is allegedly negligent is not in fact employed by the NHS Trust or practice where the treatment was provided then that Trust or practice is unlikely to be vicariously liable for his or her negligence. In these circumstances it has been recognised that so-called "umbrella" liability of the Trust or practice might arise, *i.e.* that the Trust or practice may be directly and primarily liable to the patient to ensure that treatment is not negligently provided. This is a new and unique species of liability but it has been recognised in principle in England: see *Robertson v Nottingham HA* [1997] 8 Med. L.R. 1, CA and *M v Caulderdale and Kirklees HA* [1998] Lloyd's Rep. Med. 157. However, the scope of this authority was recently called into question by the Court of Appeal in *A v MOD* [2004] EWCA Civ 641 where there was held to be no "umbrella" liability in relation to an MOD hospital in Germany.
  (For the relevant pleading of a direct non-delegable duty see precedent 72–S1.)
  (3) English courts have also clearly recognised that hospitals (whether private or NHS) have a duty to provide a safe system of providing healthcare. This is another form of primary duty of care owed to patients. It should be specifically pleaded so as to include reference to the respects in which it is alleged that the defendant failed in this duty.
  (4) Where healthcare is provided in the private sector the claim should be formulated in both contract and tort. The correct contracting party must be identified. It should be remembered that the court will be very reluctant to imply any guarantee of successful treatment (see *Thake v Maurice*). Indeed in most cases the duty of care in tort is co-extensive with the contractual duty implied. However, a claim in contract may have other advantages from the point of view of limitation or quantum.
  (For a pleading in both contract and tort see 72–S2.)
  (5) The courts approach the issue of breach of duty in cases of clinical negligence by reference to the *Bolam* test, *i.e.* the test formulated by McNair J. in his direction to the jury in *Bolam v Friern Hospital Management Committee* [1957] 1 W.L.R. 582. The effect of the *Bolam* test, as interpreted in the House of Lords in *Bolitho*, is that the defendant must live up to the standard of the ordinary skilled man exercising and professing to have that special skill, and should not be found to be negligent if he has acted in accordance with a practice accepted as proper by a responsible body of medical men skilled in the particular art. The existence of the practice is not of itself determinative of the question of negligence. The court has to subject the evidence from medical expert witnesses to scrutiny and analysis in order to decide whether it establishes that the practice or decision of the defendant was reasonable. The issue of reasonableness is ultimately for the court and not for the expert witnesses.

(6) One particular area in which clinical negligence cases differ from other personal injury claims is in respect of claims that the negligence consisted in a failure to provide the patient (or possibly another person) with relevant information about the procedure to be informed, usually information as to risks and/or side-effects. The leading case is *Sidaway v Board of Governors of the Bethlem Hospital* [1985] A.C. 871. *Sidaway* was recently considered and approved in *Pearce v United Bristol Healthcare NHS Trust* (1999) 48 B.M.L.R. 118. Essentially, the law appears to be that the test for negligence is the same as for negligence in treatment cases save that a court will find the defendant liable if it is found that the relevant information was necessary for the patient to make a balanced decision whether or not to undergo treatment.

(7) Since *Bolitho v City & Hackney Health Authority* [1997] 3 W.L.R. 1151, HL, it has been open to a claimant in a clinical negligence action involving an allegedly negligent failure to take a particular step to prove causation in one of two ways. First, by showing that if the defendant had not been negligent the claimant would, on a balance of probabilities, have been provided with the treatment which would have avoided his ultimate injury. Secondly, and if it is not possible to succeed on the first argument, that if the defendant had not been negligent and the claimant had subsequently been treated with all reasonable care that the claimant's ultimate injury would have been avoided. The situation in *Bolitho* was that the claimant in that case (the claimant had died by the time the case reached the House of Lords at which time his claim was continued by his mother as his personal representative) argued that the defendant's failure to attend when called was negligent (which was accepted by the defendant) and that if the relevant doctor had attended she would and/or should have intubated him which was accepted as being the only step which could have avoided his ultimate respiratory arrest. The doctor's evidence was that she would not have intubated him and the defendant's evidence was that that failure to intubate would not have been negligent. Accordingly, in *Bolitho* the "second bite of the cherry" argument as to causation was that the claimant should succeed if the court were to find that the failure to intubate would have been negligent notwithstanding the trial judge's finding that the doctor would not have intubated. The House of Lords accepted that this argument was available in principle but found on the facts that a failure to intubate would not have been negligent. It is not known precisely how the "two bites of the cherry argument" as to causation would apply where the party who it is alleged ought to have taken steps to avoid the claimant's injury is someone other than the defendant, for example, where the clinical negligence claim is against a GP for failure to refer a patient to a specialist and the enquiry for causation is whether or not the specialist would and/or should have diagnosed the claimant's condition.

The Court of Appeal has clearly stated that if so-called "*Bolitho*" causation arguments are to be run, *i.e.* causation is to be argued in the alternative, then it should be expressly pleaded so as the defendant is able to formulate his defence.

(The relevant statement of claim dealing with these alternative arguments as to causation is at 72–S5.)

(8) Causation in cases of delay in providing treatment or diagnosis must be approached in accordance with the guidance from the courts as set out in *Tahir v Haringay* [1998] Lloyd's Rep. Med. 104, namely that the evidence must establish an identifiable injury caused by the negligence and it is insufficient merely to plead, or prove, that the alleged negligence "made matters worse". Further guidance on causation in cases of delay was provided by the House of Lords in *Hotson v East Berkshire Health Authority* [1987] A.C. 750 where it was held, on the facts of that case, that damages were not recoverable for loss of a chance of full recovery, as in that particular case, the evidence was that as at the time of the negligence the claimant did not have a chance of recovery as such. Rather, the evidence established that as at that time he would either have recovered, or not, and the difficulty was in ascertaining which category he would have been in.

(9) Recent House of Lords decisions have confirmed that:

(a) As a matter of policy, although not as a matter of traditional principles of causation, a claimant should be entitled to recover if she can establish that, but for the negligence of the defendant, she would not have consented to surgery taking place at the identical time and place, and the risk about which she should have been warned eventuated—*Chester v Afshar* [2004] UKHL 41. The relevant particulars of claim dealing with this argument is at 72–S6.1.

(b) There can be no damages for loss of a chance of achieving a better outcome, or of avoiding a particular injury. Rather, all injury must be shown on the balance of probabilities to have been caused by the defendant's negligence. It is therefore necessary in pleading and in evidence to ensure that the causal link between the alleged negligence and the injury is fully articulated—*Gregg v Scott* [2005] UKHL 2.

(10) Limitation may cause difficulties in clinical negligence cases. Patients may well expect to have unsuccessful clinical treatment and/or side effects. Accordingly, it will often not be readily apparent to them that they have suffered an "injury" as such. Accordingly, particular care is needed when considering knowledge for the purposes of s.14 of the Limitation Act 1980.

(The relevant pleading of knowledge for limitation as at 72–S6.)

Defences

Add after para.72–05:

It was the custom in the past to plead a general denial in actions for professional negligence. However, the present practice is to plead any affirmative defence. This is required by the new rules (CPR r.16.5(2)). Therefore, the defence should reflect the case arising on the defendants' expert and/or witness evidence as it stands at the date of service of the defence. The attitude of openness reflected in and required by the Pre-action Protocol for the Resolution of Clinical Disputes suggests also that defendants in clinical negligence claims should, if at all possible, plead their positive case in the defence. The early identification of issues encouraged by the Protocol should make it easier for defendants to conduct their own investigations of the matters alleged by the claimant well before the time for service of the defence. It may, however, be that later amendments may be required as the expert evidence is developed in response to the precise allegations in the particulars of claim.

72–06

Further, the courts expect "candid disclosure" from a professional man in professional negligence cases, in particular medical negligence claims. Lord Donaldson M.R. in *Naylor v Preston AHA* [1987] 1 W.L.R. 958 expressly stated that:

"The rules require such [an affirmative] case to be pleaded. If it is not pleaded the judge may not allow it to be made or may severely penalise the defendants in costs. If late application is made to amend to plead such a case, leave may be refused in the absence of an explanation of why it was not done sooner or again the defendants may be severely penalised in costs."

An affirmative case arises when:

(a) a duty of care to a particular claimant or class is denied, for example because the claimant was not in a doctor-patient relationship with the defendant at the material time;
(b) the facts alleging breach of duty are disputed;
(c) it is alleged that the defendants acted in accordance with a responsible body of opinion within their profession and that that practice stands up to analysis (*Bolitho*);
(d) causation is disputed, *e.g.* the plaintiff's condition arose from a separate cause unrelated to the alleged negligence;
(e) causation is disputed in a case involving an allegedly negligent omission on the basis that it is denied that, if the relevant action had been taken the injury would or should have been prevented in any event;

(f) *novus actus interveniens* is relied upon;
(g) even if negligence is proved the plaintiff would have contracted the medical condition alleged, or suffered a real loss in any event;
(h) a supervening but unrelated medical condition has arisen reducing the extent of the plaintiff's claim for damages (*Jobling v Associated Dairies Ltd* [1982] A.C. 794); or
(i) as a matter of causation it is pleaded that, on the balance of probabilities, the patient would have had the surgery at the same time, or would have sustained the same injury whenever the surgery took place, or that the negligence did not lead to any increased risk.

Add after 72–S6:

72–S6.1   Pleading positive case as to causation on the basis of Chester v Afshar

Particulars of Claim

1. At all material times the Defendant owned, managed and administered the [hospital] ("the Hospital") pursuant to the provisions of the National Health Service Acts, and provided, medical, specialist and other services including [ ] services.

2. The Defendant owed a duty of care to the Claimant in relation to [his treatment], including all matters arising out of or incidental thereto. Without limiting the generality of this duty, the duty of care comprised the following:

    (a) a direct, non-delegable duty of care to ensure that reasonable care was at all times taken in relation to the medical, nursing and other care with which the Claimant was provided by or on behalf of the Hospital; and

    (b) a duty at all time to take reasonable care to ensure that there was a safe system of health care provided at the Hospital. This duty comprised [ ].

3. The Defendant its servants or agents owed a duty of care to the Plaintiff to act with reasonable skill and care when advising and/or treating him.

4. The Defendant employed or engaged the medical, surgical, nursing and other staff who worked in the Hospital and, accordingly, the Defendant is also liable in respect of any breach of duty or negligence on their part.

5. On or about [set out history of development of condition/treatment (including references to medical records or nursing notes where relevant)].

    (a) [ ]
    (b) [ ]

6. The matters set out above were caused by the negligence of the Defendant its servants or agents.

Particulars of Negligence

    (a) [set out particulars of failure to warn]
    (b) [ ]

(c) in all the circumstances failing to provide a safe system for the provision of health care. For the avoidance of doubt it is the Plaintiff's case that such a system should have included:

(i) [   ]

7. By reason of the above the Plaintiff has suffered pain injury loss and damage.

8. For the avoidance of doubt, the Claimant's case will be that:

(a) If the Claimant had been informed of the risk of [   ] then he would not have consented to the surgery taking place on [date];

(b) He would have [further considered his options]/[sought a second opinion];

(c) His injury occurred by reason of the occurrence of the risk of [   ] which was within the scope of the duty owed to him by the Defendant, and breached as particularised above;

(d) In the circumstances, the Defendant caused the injuries from which the Claimant suffers.

Particulars of Loss and Damage

The Plaintiff was born on [DOB] and is now aged [   ] years.

The Plaintiff's work, hobbies, social, recreational and other activities have been adversely affected [*NB. delete as appropriate*].

The Plaintiff may in the future require [   ].

The Plaintiff's claim includes a claim for handicap on the open labour market/the cost of care which his wife has provided gratuitously to him on account of his injuries [delete one or both as appropriate].

Full particulars of the injuries, treatment and prognosis are set out in the reports of [   ] served with this Particulars of Claim.

The calculation of this claim is set out in the Schedule of Damage served with this Particulars of Claim.

9. The Plaintiff's claim includes a claim for interest pursuant to s.69 of the County Courts Act 1984 for such periods and at such rates as the Court thinks fit.

THE PLAINTIFF CLAIMS:

(1) damages in excess of [   ];

(2) interest thereon pursuant to s.69 of the County Courts Act 1984 at such rate and for such periods as the Court thinks fit.

Insert after 72–S13:

Defence of NHS Trust and/or individual doctor setting out positive case as to causation in case pleaded on the basis of Chester v Afshar

Defence

72–S14

1. Paragraph 1 of the Particulars of Claim is admitted.

2. The Defendant admits that a duty of care was owed in the circumstances alleged but makes no admissions as to the scope or content of the duty.

3. It is admitted that the Defendant employed [   ] but as set out below it is denied that [   ] was negligent in the circumstances. Accordingly, it is denied that the Defendant is vicariously liable as alleged.

4. As to paragraphs 4–10 of the Particulars of Claim:
   (a) Set out in detail the Defendant's case as to the factual matters alleged, including references to medical records where appropriate;
   (b) [   ]
   (c) [   ]
   (d) Other than as set out above the matters set out in paragraphs 4–10 are neither admitted nor denied. They are not within the Defendant's knowledge and the Claimant is put to strict proof of these matters.

5. It is denied that the Defendant its servants or agents were negligent whether as alleged or at all or that the Claimant suffered any injury by reason thereof.

6. It is denied that the Claimant suffered any injury by reason of any negligence on the part of the Defendant and/or by reason of the treatment provided by the Defendant.

7. Further and without prejudice to the above denial it is the Defendant's case that the Claimant would have consented to the treatment provided even if the Defendant had told the Claimant [   ]. At the time of the proposed treatment the Claimant was suffering from [   ]. The Claimant's personal and professional life was seriously affected by this condition. The Claimant told the Defendant [   ]. In the light of these matters it is denied that it is more likely than not that the Claimant would have refused the treatment and/or delayed the treatment even if the Defendant had told the Claimant [   ].

8. Further or in the alternative, if and when the Claimant did undergo the treatment the likelihood is that he would have suffered the same injury as he ultimately suffered.

9. [continue as for personal injury defence]

Part T

PROFESSIONAL NEGLIGENCE

Section 75: Professional Negligence

Duty of care
Add at end:

Recent case law has recognised that it is impossible to reconcile all the judicial statements on the correct methodology to be applied to novel situations in which a person is alleged to owe a duty of care to another, and that the courts should take a more cautious approach to imposing that duty where economic loss is claimed than in relation to physical damage. The appropriate course for ascertaining whether there is a duty of care in an economic loss case is to look at any new set of facts by using each of the three approaches namely, the threefold test, the voluntary assumption of responsibility test and the incremental test: see, for example, *Commissioners for Customs and Excise v Barclays Bank Plc* [2004] EWCA Civ 1555; [2005] 1 Lloyd's Rep. 165, CA.

75–02

Causation and loss
Delete the fourth sentence and replace with:

Thus the mere fact that a negligent audit of a company's account which showed profits when they should have showed losses had the effect of enabling the company to remain trading (*i.e.* "but for" the negligence it would have stopped trading) does not mean that the auditors were liable for all the losses consequent upon that continued trading.

75–04

Add after second paragraph:

The normal rule requiring proof that the negligence complained of caused the injury was modified by a majority of the House of Lords in *Chester v Afshar* [2004] UKHL 41; [2005] 1 A.C. 134. The defendant surgeon had negligently failed to warn the claimant that the intended operation carried a 1–2 per cent risk of neurological injury, which in fact occurred in her case. If she had been warned, there was no finding on the balance of probabilities that she would not have had the operation. On normal principles she could not establish causation but the importance of her right to be fully informed denied her by the defendant meant that he should still be responsible for her losses as they fell within the scope of his duty to warn.

In the context of clinical negligence, where the defendant negligently failed to advise the claimant to have an examination so that diagnosis of cancer was delayed by a year, by which time it had advanced, a majority of the House of Lords held in *Gregg v Scott* [2005] UKHL 2; [2005] 2 A.C. 176 that the claimant could not establish causation where, at the time when he should have been diagnosed, he only had a 42 per cent chance of cure (surviving more than 10 years) even though by the time of actual diagnosis this had reduced to 25 per cent. Proof of causation on a balance of probabilities was required and could not be substituted by a lesser award to reflect the lower prospects of cure analogous to the "loss of a chance" cases.

Claim for damages for negligence against auditors
Replace paragraph 2. with:

2. By an agreement made between the Claimant and the Defendants contained or evidenced in an engagement letter dated [date] [*or as the case may be*] the Defendants agreed to act as auditors to the Claimant in consideration of the payment of their fees ("the Agreement").

75–T1

Defence relying on limitation in clinical negligence

Replace with:

75–T14 The injury complained of occurred, if at all, on [date], such date being more than three years before the issue of the Claim Form herein and the claim is therefore barred by s.11 of the Limitation Act 1980.

[Statement of truth]

Part U
PROPERTY

SECTION 78: BUSINESS TENANCIES

General.

Add after first sentence:

The law has recently been amended by the Regulatory Reform (Business Tenancies) (England and Wales) Order 2003 (SI 2003/3096), which came into force on June 1, 2004. Transitional provisions provide, *inter alia*, that where before June 1, 2004 a landlord has given notice under s.25 of the Act or the tenant has made a request for a new tenancy under s.26, nothing in the Order has effect in relation to the notice or request or anything done in consequence of it.

78–01

Lease renewals.

Delete text from "If a landlord serves a s.25 notice" to the end of the paragraph, and replace with:

Upon service of a s.25 or s.26 notice a landlord or tenant may apply to court for a new tenancy under s.24(1). A landlord may apply to the court for the determination of the continuation tenancy without the grant of a new tenancy if he has given a s.25 notice or a counter-notice to a tenant's s.26 notice opposing the grant of a new tenancy provided that the notice or counter-notice states that the landlord is opposed to the grant of a new tenancy on one or more of the grounds in s.30 of the Act (s.29(2)).

Save where the parties agree otherwise, s.29A sets out the time limits for applications to court. An application by the landlord or tenant pursuant to s.24(1) of the Act or an application by the landlord s.26 request must not be made before the end of the period of two months beginning with the date of the making of the request, unless the application is made after a landlord's s.26 counter-notice.

78–02

Interim rent.

Replace paragraph with:

Section 24A of the Act permits a landlord or tenant to apply for an interim rent following a landlord's notice to terminate the tenancy under s.25 or a tenant's request for a new tenancy while a tenancy is continued by virtue of s.24. The application must be made before the expiry of six months after the termination of the former tenancy. Upon such an application the court may order payment of an interim rent in accordance with s.24C or 24D of the Act. The interim rent is payable from the "appropriate date", *i.e.* the earliest date that could have been specified in the s.25 notice or s.26 request.

78–03

Exclusion of provisions of Part II of the Landlord and Tenant Act 1954.

Replace second sentence with:

Section 38A provides that the persons who will be landlord and tenant in relation to a business tenancy to be granted for a term of years may agree that the provisions of ss.24 to 28 of the Act will be excluded in relation to that tenancy or make an agreement to surrender provided that certain procedural requirements are met. The requirement that the court should authorise any exclusion by agreement has been removed.

78–04

Compensation upon termination of tenancy.

Replace last sentence of first paragraph with:

This is payable by the landlord where that landlord has served a notice under s.25 or a counter-notice to a s.26 request opposing the grant of a new tenancy on grounds (e), (f) or

78–05

(g) of s.30(1) and no others and (a) the tenant does not apply to court for a new tenancy or (b) the tenant withdraws his application or (c) the tenant applies to court and the court is precluded from ordering the grant of a new tenancy by one of those grounds and no other (s.30(1), (1A), (1B) and (1C)).

Compensation is also payable where the landlord obtains an order for possession or the tenant quits the holding by reason of misrepresentation or concealment of material facts.

Add at end of second paragraph:

If those conditions are satisfied in relation to part of the holding only, the compensation is the aggregate of sums calculated separately as compensation in respect of each part (s.37(3A)). Provision is also made for cases where the reversion is divided between different landlords (s.37(3B)).

Proceedings

Replace first sentence of second paragraph with:

78–06 Landlord and tenant claims are brought using the procedure in CPR Pt 8 as modified by CPR Pt 56, save where the claim is for a new tenancy under s.24 of the Act in circumstances where the grant of a new tenancy is opposed or for the termination of a tenancy under s.29(2) of the Act in which event the appropriate procedure is that in CPR Pt 7 as modified by CPR Pt 56.

Lease Renewals

Replace first paragraph and list with:

78–07 In both opposed and unopposed claims the claim form must contain details of—
(a) the property to which the claim relates;
(b) the particulars of the current tenancy (including date, parties and duration), the current rent (if not the original rent) and the date and method of termination;
(c) every notice or request made under s.25 or 26 of the Act; and
(d) the expiry date of—
 (i) the statutory period under s.29A(2) of the Act; or
 (ii) any agreed extended period made under s.29B(1) or 29B(2) of the Act (PD56, para.3.4).

Where the claimant is the tenant making a claim for a new tenancy under s.24 of the Act, in addition the claim form must contain details of—
(a) the nature of the business carried on at the property;
(b) whether the claimant relies on s.23(1A), 41 or 42 of the Act and, if so, the basis on which he does so;
(c) whether any, and if so what part, of the property comprised in the tenancy is occupied neither by the claimant nor by a person employed by the claimant for the purpose of the claimant's business;
(d) the claimant's proposed terms of the new tenancy; and
(e) the name and address of—
 (i) anyone known to the claimant who has an interest in the reversion in the property (whether immediate or in not more than 15 years) on the termination of the claimant's current tenancy and who is likely affected by the grant of a new tenancy;
 (ii) if the claimant does not know of anyone with such an interest, anyone who has a freehold in the property (PD56, para.3.5) (a copy of the claim form must also be served on any person so named (PD56, para.3.6)).

Where the claimant is the landlord making a claim for a new tenancy under s.24 of the Act, in addition the claim form must contain details of—
(a) the claimant's proposed terms of the new tenancy;

(b) whether the claimant is aware that the defendant's tenancy is one to which s.32(2) of the Act applies and, if so, whether the claimant requires that any new tenancy shall be a tenancy of the whole of the property comprised in the current tenancy or just of the holding as defined by s.23(3) of the Act; and
(c) the name and address of—
   (i) anyone known to the claimant who has an interest in the reversion in the property (whether immediate or in not more than 15 years) on the termination of the claimant's current tenancy and who is likely affected by the grant of a new tenancy;
   (ii) if the claimant does not know of anyone with such an interest, anyone who has a freehold in the property (PD56, para.3.7) (a copy of the claim form must also be served on any person so named (PD56, para.3.8)).

Where the claimant is the landlord making an application for the termination of a tenancy under s.29(2) of the Act, in addition the claim form must contain details of—
(a) the claimant's grounds of opposition;
(b) full details of those grounds of opposition; and
(c) the terms of a new tenancy that the claimant proposes in the event that his claim fails (PD56, para.3.9).

Add at beginning of what was the second paragraph:

In all cases,

Delete text from what was the third paragraph to the end of p.1317, and replace with:

Where the claim is an opposed claim and the claimant is the tenant, the acknowledgment of service must be in Form N210 and must state with particulars—
(a) whether, if a new tenancy is granted, the defendant objects to any of the terms proposed by the claimant and, if so—
   (i) the terms to which he objects; and
   (ii) the terms that he proposes insofar as they differ from those proposed by the claimant;
(b) whether the defendant is a tenant under a lease having less than 15 years unexpired at the date of the termination of the claimant's current tenancy and, if so, the name and address of any person who, to the knowledge of the defendant, has an interest in the reversion of the property expectant (whether immediate or in not more than 15 years from that date) on the termination of the defendant's tenancy;
(c) the name and address of any person having an interest in the property who is likely to be affected by the grant of a new tenancy; and
(d) if the claimant's current tenancy is one to which s.32(2) of the Act applies, whether the defendant requires that any new tenancy shall be a tenancy of the whole of the property comprised in the claimant's current tenancy.

Where the claim is an unopposed claim and the claimant is the landlord, the acknowledgment of service must be in Form N210 and must state with particulars—
(a) the nature of the business carried on at the property;
(b) if the defendant relies on s.23(1A), 41 or 42 of the Act, the basis on which he does so;
(c) whether any, and if so what part, of the property comprised in the tenancy is occupied neither by the tenant nor by a person employed by the defendant for the purposes of the defendant's business;
(d) the name and address of—
   (i) anyone known to the claimant who has an interest in the reversion in the property (whether immediate or in not more than 15 years) on the termination of the claimant's current tenancy and who is likely affected by the grant of a new tenancy;
   (ii) if the claimant does not know of anyone with such an interest, anyone who has a freehold in the property;

(e) whether, if a new tenancy is granted, the defendant objects to any of the terms proposed by the claimant and, if so—
  (i) the terms to which he objects; and
  (ii) the terms that he proposes insofar as they differ from those proposed by the claimant (PD56, para.3.11).

Where a claim is an opposed claim and the claimant is the tenant the acknowledgment of service must be in Form N9 and, in his defence, the defendant must state with particulars—
  (a) the defendant's grounds of opposition;
  (b) full details of those grounds of opposition;
  (c) whether, if a new tenancy is granted, the defendant objects to any of the terms proposed by the claimant and, if so—
    (i) the terms to which he objects; and
    (ii) the terms that he proposes insofar as they differ from those proposed by the claimant;
  (d) whether the defendant is a tenant under a lease having less than 15 years unexpired at the date of the termination of the current tenancy and, if so, the name and address of any person who, to the knowledge of the defendant, has an interest in the reversion in the property expectant (whether immediately or in not more than 15 years from that date) on the termination of the tenancy;
  (e) the name and address of any person having an interest in the property who is likely to be affected by the grant of a new tenancy; and
  (f) if the claimant's current tenancy is one to which s.32(2) of the Act applies, whether the defendant requires that any new tenancy shall be a tenancy of the whole of the property comprised in the current tenancy (PD56, para.3.12).

Where the claim is an opposed claim and the claimant is the landlord the acknowledgment of service must be in Form N9 and the defendant must, in his defence, state with particulars—
  (a) whether the defendant relies on s.23(1A), 41 or 42 of the Act and, if so, the basis on which he does so;
  (b) whether the defendant relies on s.31A of the Act and, if so, the basis on which he does so; and
  (c) the terms of the new tenancy that the defendant would propose in the event that the claim to terminate the current tenancy fails (PD56, para.3.13).

Replace last two paragraphs with:

Where the claim is an unopposed claim, no evidence need be filed unless and until the court directs it to be filed. Where the claim is an opposed claim evidence (including expert evidence) must be filed by the parties as the court directs and the landlord must in any event file his evidence first (PD56, paras 3.14 and 3.15).

Unless in the circumstances it is unreasonable to do so, any grounds of opposition shall be tried as a preliminary issue (PD56, para.3.16).

Interim Rent

Replace with:

78–08 Where proceedings have been commenced an application for interim rent may be made by the claim form, the acknowledgment of service or defence or application notice under CPR Pt 23 (in Form N244). Where no proceedings have been commenced or proceedings have been commenced but disposed of the application must be made under CPR Pt 8 (in Form N208) and the claim form must include details of—
  (a) the property to which the claim relates;
  (b) the particulars of the relevant tenancy (including date, parties and duration) and the current rent (if not the original rent);
  (c) every notice or request given or made under s.25 or 26 of the Act;

(d) if the relevant tenancy has been terminated, the date and mode of termination; and
(e) if the relevant tenancy has been terminated and the landlord has granted a new tenancy of the property to the tenant—
   (i) particulars of the new tenancy (including date, parties and duration) and the rent; and
   (ii) in a case where s.24C(2) of the Act applies but the claimant seeks a different rent under s.24C(3) of the Act, particulars and matters on which the claimant relies as satisfying s.24C(3).

Form 78–U1 is redundant in relation to claims made following the service of notice after June 1, 2004. **78–U1**

Replace 78–U2 with:

Unopposed application by tenant for new business tenancy (Claim under CPR Pt 8) 78–U2

This claim [includes] [does not include] any issues under the Human Rights Act 1998.

Details of Claim

1. [I] [We] [ ] of [ ] apply to the court for the grant of a new tenancy pursuant to s.24 of the Landlord and Tenant Act 1954.

2. The premises to which this application relates are: [Give address of premises].

3. The nature of the business carried on at the premises is:

4. The following are the particulars of [my] [our] current tenancy of the premises:
   (a) (Date of lease or agreement for a lease or tenancy agreement)
   (b) (Names of parties to lease or agreement)
   (c) (Term granted by lease or agreement)
   (d) (Rent reserved by lease or agreement)
   (e) (Terms as to date and mode of termination of tenancy)
   (f) (Whether any, and if so, what part of the property comprised in the tenancy is occupied neither by the tenant, nor by a person employed by the tenant for the purposes of the business carried on by the tenant in the premises)

5. [I] [We] do not rely upon s.23(1A), 41 or 42 of the Landlord and Tenant Act 1954.

6. On [date] the Defendant served on [me] [us] a notice to terminate dated [date] in accordance with the provisions of s.25 of the Landlord and Tenant Act 1954 specifying [date] as the date for termination and stating that the Defendant would not oppose an application to this court for a new tenancy.

Or

On [date] [I] [we] served on the Defendant a request dated [date] for a new tenancy in accordance with the provisions of s.26 of the Landlord and Tenant Act 1954 specifying [date] as the date for commencement of the new tenancy.

The Defendant has not served on [me] [us] any counter-notice.

7. The claim is unopposed, therefore [I] [we] do not rely upon s.31A of the Landlord and Tenant Act 1954.

8. The expiry date of the statutory period under s.29A(2) of the Landlord and Tenant Act 1954 is [date].

9. [I] [We] have not agreed an extended period under s.29B(1) or 29B(2) of the Landlord and Tenant Act 1954.

10. The following are [my] [our] proposals as to the period, rent and other terms of the new tenancy for which [I am] [we are] applying:

11. The following persons are to [my] [our] knowledge interested in the reversion in the premises on the termination of [my] [our] tenancy:

[Give names and addresses and nature of interest in the premises (whether immediately or in not more than 15 years), of persons likely to be affected by the grant of a new tenancy *or* of anyone who has a freehold interest in the property.]

12. The name and address of the Defendant on whom this application is intended to be served are:

13. [My] [Our] address for service is:

14. Part 8 of the Civil Procedure Rules 1998 applies to this claim.

[Statement of truth]

Replace 78–U4 with:

78–U4   **Defence to application for new business tenancy in respect of a tenancy to which s.32 of the Landlord and Tenant Act 1954 applies, including an application for interim rent pursuant to s.24 thereof**

1. The Defendant admits paragraphs [   ] of the Particulars of Claim.

2. The Defendant opposes the grant of a new tenancy on the following grounds stated in his notice under section [25] [26(6)] of the Landlord and Tenant Act 1954, namely:

(Set out grounds of opposition)

3. The details of those grounds of opposition are as follows:

(Set out full details of grounds)

4. [If a new tenancy is granted, the Defendant does not object to its being granted on the terms proposed by the Claimant.

Or

[If a new tenancy is granted, the Defendant objects to its being granted on the following terms proposed by the Claimant, namely:]

(Set out the terms objected to)

and the following are the Defendant's counter-proposals as to the period, rent and other terms of such new tenancy:]

Particulars of Counter-Proposals

(Set out the Defendant's counter-proposals)

5. [The Defendant is not a tenant under a lease having less than 15 years unexpired at the at the date of the termination of the Claimant's tenancy.]

Or

[The Defendant is a tenant under a lease having less than 15 years unexpired at the date of the termination of the Claimant's tenancy, and the name(s) and address(es) of the person(s) having an interest in the reversion expectant on the termination of the Defendant's tenancy immediately or in not more than 15 years of the date of such determination [is] [are]:]

Particulars of Interested Persons

(Set out the names and addresses of any reversioners)

6. The following persons are to the Defendant's knowledge likely to be affected by the grant of a new tenancy:

Particulars of Persons Likely to be Affected by Grant

(Set out the names and addresses of all persons who are likely to be affected and the nature of the interest of each such person.)

7. The Claimant's tenancy is one to which s.32(2) of the Landlord and Tenant Act 1954 applies and, accordingly, the Defendant requires that any new tenancy ordered to be granted shall be a tenancy of the whole of the property comprised in the Claimant's current tenancy.

8. The Defendant hereby applies to the Court under s.24A of the Landlord and Tenant Act 1954 to determine a rent which would be reasonable for the Claimant to pay while the tenancy continues by virtue of s.24 of the Landlord and Tenant Act 1954.

[Statement of Truth]

Particulars of Claim for possession of business premises relying on agreement to exclude ss.24 to 28 of the Landlord and Tenant Act 1954

78–U7

Replace paragraphs 4. and 5. with:

4. Before the Lease was entered into the Claimant and Defendant entered into an agreement excluding the provisions of ss.24 to 28 inclusive of the Landlord and Tenant Act 1954 pursuant to s.38A thereof.

5. Clause [ ] of the Lease makes reference to the notice served by the Claimant before the Lease was entered into and to the said agreement.

Replace title with:

Particulars of claim for possession of business premises on tenant's failure to apply to court for a new tenancy

78–U8

Replace paragraph 7. with:

7. Subsequently the Defendant did not make an application for a new tenancy before the date specified in the notice under s.25 of the Landlord and Tenant Act 1954.

Section 83: Easements and Drainage

For "Gale on Easements (16th ed., 1996)", substitute:

Gale on Easements (17th ed., 2002)   **83–01**

Rights of way

In the second paragraph, add citation to Hanning v Top Deck Travel Group Ltd:

(1994) 68 P. & C.R. 14   **83–03**

Add at end:

However there is no requirement of public policy that prevents the acquisition of an easement by long and uninterrupted use in breach of a statutory prohibition where it would have been lawful for the landowner to make such a grant and where such a grant would have removed the criminality of user: *Bakewell Management Ltd v Brandwood* [2004] UKHL 14; [2004] 2 W.L.R. 955.

Section 84: Fences, Boundaries and Access to Neighbouring Land

Boundary disputes

Delete second and third sentences and replace with:

The courts had a general power to order the rectification of a register of title where appropriate: see ss.82 and 138 of the Land Registration Act 1925. Changes brought into force by the Land Registration Act 2002 mean that the power of rectification has been changed to that of "alteration": Land Registration Act 2002, s.65 and Sch.4.

84–03

Boundary Disputes

Particulars of Claim in boundary dispute seeking declaration as to ownership of registered land and alteration of the Land Register

Replace paragraph 8. with:

8. The Claimant applies for alteration of title number [   ] pursuant to ss.82 and 138 of the Land Registration Act 1925.

84–U3

SECTION 86: LANDLORD AND TENANT—OTHER COVENANTS

Quiet Enjoyment.
Add at end:

; *Southwark London Borough Council v Mills* [1999] 4 All E.R. 449, HL   **86–05**

Section 87: Landlord and Tenant—Flats

Replace penultimate sentence with:

The Landlord and Tenant Act 1985 is most recently amended by the Commonhold and Leasehold Reform Act 2002, the relevant provisions of which are now mostly in force. **87–01**

Delete last sentence of second paragraph. **87–04**

Part 8 Claim Form Details of Claim seeking declaration that premises are excluded premises for the purposes of s.1 of the Landlord and Tenant Act 1987

In paragraphs 1.(1)(a) and 1.(1)(b), for "500f", substitute:
   (b) 50 per cent of **87–U1**

Application to the Leasehold Valuation Tribunal seeking the appointment of a manager pursuant to Part II of the Landlord and Tenant Act 1987 **87–U7**

Add footnote to the title:

Note 1: Where the application is made or proceedings transferred to a LVT on or after September 30, 2003 (England) or March 31, 2004 (Wales), it must comply with the requirements of the Commonhold and Leasehold Reform Act 2002, ss.173 to 176 and Sch.12 and the Leasehold Valuation Tribunals (Procedure) (England) Regulations 2003 (SI 2003/2099) or the Leasehold Valuation Tribunals (Procedure) (Wales) Regulations 2004 (SI 2004/681 (W.69)).

In the title, for "s.42", substitute:
s.13 **87–U10**

SECTION 88: LANDLORD AND TENANT—POSSESSION PROCEEDINGS

Common Law Claims

Particulars of Claim by landlord claiming possession of business premises, relying on agreement to exclude sections 24 to 28 of the Landlord and Tenant Act 1954

Replace paragraphs 4. and 5. with:

4. Before the Lease was entered into the Claimant and Defendant entered into an agreement excluding the provisions of ss.24 to 28 inclusive of the Landlord and Tenant Act 1954 pursuant to s.38A thereof.

5. Clause [   ] of the Lease makes reference to the notice served by the Claimant before the Lease was entered into and to the said agreement.

88–U10

SECTION 90: LANDLORD AND TENANT—RENT AND SERVICE CHARGES

Replace fifth sentence of second paragraph with:

The Commonhold and Leasehold Reform Act 2002 substitutes s.20 with new ss.20 and 20ZA under which consultation requirements are prescribed by the Service Charges (Consultation Requirements) (England) Regulations 2003 (SI 2003/1987). **90–02**

Section 94: Mortgages and Charges

Pleadings points for a mortgage claim

Transitional cases.

In relation to the first paragraph, RSC Order 88 (transitional cases) is no longer in force. **94–07**

Section 96: Sale of Land

Options and Rights of Pre-emption.

Delete last two sentences in second paragraph and replace with:

The law relating to rights of pre-emption in respect of registered land has, however, been fundamentally altered by s.115 of the Land Registration Act 2002. Under s.115 of that Act any such right created on or after that section came into force (October 13, 2003: Land Registration Act (Commencement No.4) Order 2003) has effect from the time of creation as an interest capable of binding successors in title (subject to the rules on the effect of dispositions on priority). **96–09**

Section 97: Trespass to Land

Trespass.

Replace second paragraph with:

For the provisions as to limitation of the right to recover possession of land in unregistered and registered land see Section 77: Adverse Possession. **97–01.2**

Replace title with:

Defence claiming title to unregistered land by adverse possession   97–U4

Replace paragraph 1. with:

1. The Defendant admits that the Claimant was formerly the freehold owner of Blackacre ("the Premises") and avers that title to the Premises is unregistered.

Part V

RESTITUTION

Section 98: Restitution

Add at end of note 3:

Even if he has not realised the financial value of the benefit and has no intention of doing so, a defendant who has received a benefit which is readily returnable but who chooses not to retransfer it on request can hardly deny that he has been enriched by it: *Cressman v Coys of Kensington (Sales) Ltd* [2004] EWCA Civ 47 at [37]–[40]; [2004] 1 W.L.R. 2775 at 2791A–2792C.

98–01

Restitution for wrongs

In note 34, for "The Times, April 19, 2003", substitute:

[2003] 1 All E.R. (Comm) 830

98–07.1

Add at end of note 34:

See Burrows, *Remedies for Torts and Breach of Contract* (3rd ed., 2004), pp.405–407.

Defences

In note 36, for "[2002] 1 All E.R. 198 at 218c", substitute:

[2002] Q.B. 1286 at 1308G

98–08

Add at end of note 38:

This statement was endorsed on appeal: [2003] EWCA Civ 1446 at [164]; [2004] Q.B. 985 at 1004E. In *Barros Mattos Junior v MacDaniels Ltd* [2004] EWHC 1188; [2005] 1 W.L.R. 247, Ch, Laddie J. held on a summary judgment application that defendants who were assumed for the purposes of the application to have been "wholly innocent of the illicit source of the funds supplied to them" but whose change of position consisted in paying those funds away in transactions which were illegal in Nigeria under Nigerian foreign exchange regulations were deprived in English law of the defence of change of position (by reason of the public policy of international comity): "If the recipient's actions of changing position are treated here as illegal, the court cannot take them into account. The recipient cannot put up a tainted claim to retention against the victim's untainted claim for restitution. It may be … that in some cases the illegality will be so minor as to be ignored on the *de minimis* principle. This is not such a case." The judgment has been questioned in academic commentaries (Goff & Jones, *The Law of Restitution* (1st supplement to 6th ed.), pp.114–115 and Tettenborn (2005) L.M.C.L.Q. 6) and appears doubtful. In terms of pleading a claim against such a defendant, it would be preferable to plead the defendant's illegality in the particulars of claim (thereby forcing him to plead to it) rather than in the reply.

Part W

SPORT

Section 99: Sports Law

Alternative dispute resolution.

Add at end of second sentence:

: *Athletic Union of Constantinople v National Basketball Assoc.* [2002] EWCA Civ 830 **99–04**